BOOK SALES THAT MULTIPLY

Targeting Your Ideal Reader With eBook Promotions, Paid Ads & More!

BOOK SALES THAT MULTIPLY: MARKETING FOR AUTHORS

Copyright © 2019 by Mandi Lynn

All rights reserved.

Printed in the United States of America.

No part of this book may be used or reproduced in any manner whatsoever without written permission except in the case of brief quotations embodied in critical articles or reviews.

For information contact :

Bethany Atazadeh: bethanyatazadeh@yahoo.com

Mandi Lynn: mandi@stoneridgebooks.com

Cover Design by Stone Ridge Books

Formatting by Bethany Atazadeh

ISBN: 9781078497244

First Edition: March 2019

10 9 8 7 6 5 4 3 2 1

MARKETING FOR AUTHORS

BOOK SALES THAT MULTIPLY

Targeting Your Ideal Reader With
eBook Promotions, Paid Ads & More!

MANDI LYNN
WITH BETHANY ATAZADEH

CONTENTS

FOREWORD: BY BETHANY ATAZADEH 1

INTRODUCTION: FREE VERSUS PAID MARKETING 4

CHAPTER 1: YOUR IDEAL READER 22

CHAPTER 2: CREATING GRAPHICS & SALES COPY . 37

CHAPTER 3: NEWSLETTER SWAPS & FEATURES 57

CHAPTER 4: EBOOK PROMOTION SITES 80

CHAPTER 5: GOODREADS GIVEAWAYS 93

CHAPTER 6: FACEBOOK ADS 107

CHAPTER 7: UNDERSTANDING AMAZON ADVERTISING 132

CHAPTER 8: COLLECTING DATA 152

CHAPTER 9: CREATING AN AMAZON AD 180

CHAPTER 10: OPTIMIZING AMAZON ADS 197

CHAPTER 11: CELEBRATE YOURSELF 211

RESOURCES: 215

ABOUT THE AUTHORS 221

ABOUT: MANDI 222

ABOUT: BETHANY 225

FOREWORD:
BY BETHANY ATAZADEH

YOU MIGHT'VE NOTICED by now that Mandi and I take turns writing these marketing books, depending on which of us has the most expertise on that particular subject.

Mandi and I have both branched out in a lot of different marketing directions, but when it comes to things like newsletter spotlights, Facebook (and Instagram) ads, as well as Amazon ads, I'm still a newbie, while Mandi is a pro!

I wanted to start off this book by giving her props for all the knowledge she drops here. This is marketing 2.0 in my opinion. The content in this book isn't the basics anymore, it's for when you've mastered the simpler stuff and want to take your efforts to the next level.

I honestly can't take credit for the wisdom in these pages, besides the little tidbits I contribute that I've picked up along the way.

As I helped with edits (one of the many awesome aspects of co-writing by the way, being able to exchange writing and have an extra set of editorial eyes on your work), I enjoyed approaching these topics with you, the reader, in mind. I asked Mandi a million questions, in the hopes that between

Mandi and I, we could create the most clear, concise, and confidence-boosting guide to paid advertising and book marketing possible.

If you feel like conquering paid advertising and newsletter promotion is for you, then read on and enjoy!

INTRODUCTION:
FREE VERSUS PAID MARKETING

"Don't be afraid to get creative and experiment with your marketing."

- Mike Volpe

WE SPEAK FROM experience and our own mistakes when we say that your book truly is your most valuable marketing tool. Everyone wants to market their book for free. Free marketing is great because the only thing you have to invest is your time. If something doesn't go right, you don't lose any money, you've only lost your time. However, free marketing can only do so much.

Paid marketing is taking all the efforts you've made so far and multiplying them. It can help your book reach audiences who would otherwise never find your work, and keep it selling long past its release date.

Even with the best author platform, you have to work incredibly hard to continue to sell books. A solid platform means on release day your book will likely make a lot of sales. But your platform is only so big. You can only reach so many people, so how do you extend your reach even further?

This is where paid marketing comes in and this book's entire focus is 100% book promotion whether that be free or paid. We're no longer talking about platform, having a website or subscribers. In fact, if you do paid marketing well, you don't need any of those things, but if you have *both* you'll find book sales coming easier and easier.

Now, I'm sure many of you want nothing to do with paid marketing. A lot of authors start doing paid marketing because "that person on the internet told me to." You know you should be doing it, but you aren't sure *how* to do it. Instead of doing your research and learning how each paid marketing platform works, you go in blind, invest money, and lose your money. Then you never want to pay to market your books again.

Sound familiar?

There are many ways to do paid marketing wrong.

But there are also many ways to do it right!

I'll admit, I'm not an expert. In fact, I don't think there's such thing as being an expert when it comes to knowing the ins and outs of paid marketing because it's always changing. I work in digital marketing for my full-time job and have been lucky enough to experiment with different forms of paid marketing there. However, when it comes to book marketing, I've very quickly learned there's no clear step-by-step manual. What works for one person may not work for someone else at all and vice versa. Because of this, I want to explore many different options of promoting your story. Here are some things you can expect to learn by the end of this book:

- Targeting your ideal reader
- Creating graphics and sales copy for your ads
- Newsletter swaps
- Ebook promotion websites

- Goodreads Giveaways
- Facebook/Instagram ads

   Amazon ads

By picking up this book, you've made your first investment into learning how to market your book with ads. Understanding how different marketing platforms work is the first step. Read this book and use the techniques we'll go over and see how you can market your book in an entirely new way. Most of all, be prepared to learn. Marketing is not black and white, so take it all in and don't be afraid to try new things.

The Difference Between Free and Paid Marketing

Your author platform is classified as inbound marketing. **Inbound marketing** is drawing potential readers to your books through content marketing such as social media, your website, blog, and newsletter. Also known as...free marketing! Inbound marketing means you're making the customers come to you with the content you create.

Content marketing and inbound marketing are effective because they are *non-invasive ways to sell your books*. Many writers are introverts, so you may be shy when it comes to pitching your books to strangers and trying to make sales.

But why isn't an author platform enough? Because the internet is a crowded space. So many authors are creating content online; you can be drowned out by the noise. How do you make yourself heard above all the rest?

This is where outbound marketing comes into play. **Outbound marketing** means that instead of producing content to attract customers to your books/products, you're reaching out directly to your customers through ads, promotions, or even partnerships. It's the more traditional approach to marketing, but it's the type of marketing most authors tend to avoid because they don't want to "waste" their money on ads. But waste only happens when you're unsure of what you're doing. This book is to help you understand how to set up ads effectively, and pick and choose where you should run your ads.

Inbound and outbound marketing techniques are both effective on their own, but using them together will set you up for success. You'll be able to take your few sales here and there, and multiply them into sales that grow exponentially.

Learning the Art of Traffic

Knowing how to drive traffic to your books is an extremely valuable tool. Anyone can make a post about their book on social media, but not everyone knows how to create a successful ad that will effortlessly draw hundreds to thousands of readers to their books for a low investment.

This is where outbound marketing comes into play.

Up until now, Bethany and I have mostly taught you inbound marketing techniques, meaning we've taught you how to create free content to connect with your audience. This is because the writing and reading community is a very powerful tool. Networking is *huge* as an author. But now we're going to stop waiting for our readers to come to us. We're going to go out and find them.

Paid marketing, done well, has great conversion rates, which means you have the ability to convert someone from a prospect to a customer. Your author platform and content marketing are different in the sense that you are making yourself known in the community, but people aren't necessarily looking to buy a book. Your platform is a great way to establish trust with your audience and create a connection with them, that will lead them to reading your book out of curiosity or supporting you. Your author platform also works in the sense that if you get your book in front of people's eyes enough times, then eventually they'll buy it on their own. Ads are the opposite. With ads, you craft it in the perfect way so that they click on the ad the first time they see it and buy it then and there. Other times the ads will follow the rule of 7.

The Rule of 7

This is the idea that someone needs to see your book or product seven times before they will actually buy it. This goes for both your author platform, as well as creating ads. It may seem meaningless to pay for an ad, someone to see it, but not buy it. But when you combine your ads with your author platform, you increase the times someone sees your book, thus increasing the odds that someone will buy. The more times someone sees your name and your book, the more you create name recognition and increase the chances of making a sale, even if it's not right now.

With paid advertising you don't need to have a fancy website and a long list of subscribers to make a sale, you just need to tell someone why they need to start reading your book.

When to Do Paid Ads

Most people struggle with paid ads because they don't want to invest in something they're not sure about, which is completely valid! I always suggest to people that they wait to invest in paid ads until they know what they're doing.

It's easy to boost a Facebook post about your book being on sale. The ad will get more reach than it would have without being boosted. However extended reach does not always translate into book sales. Extended reach is great, but if you're investing money into ads, you want return on your investment, also known as ROI.

ROI

With this book, one of my goals is to teach you a little bit of the marketing lingo, so here we go! **ROI** stands for return on investment. This is something you need to constantly keep in mind when you're setting up your ads. How do you know if you will make a return on your investment? If you pay $50 for an ad, will you be able to make at least $50 back in sales back? If you can't at least break even then you shouldn't do that ad, because the ROI is very poor.

How to Predict Your ROI

Making a prediction of your ROI can be difficult to do if you're doing a pay-per-click ad on Amazon or Facebook. As we go through each type of marketing option, I'll show you tips to help you predict your ROI to avoid losing money. In fact, our goal is to help you to make money. If you're investing time and money into ads, the goal shouldn't be to break even. You want more book sales, so you can make more money! If you think the ROI of an ad is low, or even a wash, consider skipping the ad or learning more about it to increase your investment in the future.

Ultimatley, you want to make your book ad an impulse buy for anyone who sees it.

Creating a Call to Action

With every ad you create, I want you to have a call to action (CTA). A **CTA** is a clear prompt or request for an action you put in your content that warrants an immediate response from whoever sees the content. By this I mean that for every ad you create, you need a clear CTA that will cause someone to want to click the ad right away and buy your book. It could be as simple as "buy now" or "learn more." Create a message so compelling that they don't want to stop and think about their purchase. They just make it. Your CTA encourages an impulse buy.

Graphics and Sales Copy

Besides ROI and CTA, one of the most important things when it comes to your ads is the graphic and sales copy. This is truly what makes the sale. The **graphic** is the image that you use to sell the book, while **sales copy** is the text you use to accompany the graphic. Your graphic and sales copy is something you'll need to play around with to find what works best because it is such a vital element of making the sale. You'll also need to adjust it to fit the platform the ad is on. The graphic you use for Facebook versus a newsletter will be different. As will the sales copy. Nothing is one size fits all, and you'll learn that as we work through the chapters.

Running One Ad at a Time

Sometimes you may get eager to make sales. You'll be ready to invest and see the numbers come in. While having multiple ads running at once can feel great when you're making sales, it can be counterproductive to predicting your ROI. How do you know which ad is making you the most money if you're running three ads at once? Your ad for Facebook could be losing you money while the ad on Amazon could be making you a lot, but it would be hard to tell right away which one is selling more books because you're running multiple ads at once.

Prepare to Make Changes

Paid ads are all about learning and shifting. You're constantly making changes to get the most bang for your buck. Take your time and try not to get discouraged. Sometimes it can take only a week or two to create an ad that converts to sales, and other times it can take a month or two. I'm still adjusting an ad for my debut novel, *I am Mercy*, to determine the best way to market the book, but I have the skills and knowledge to adjust the sales copy and targeting until the ad is effective.

Is it Too Soon to Run an Ad?

When should you start running ads for your book? You can start as soon as your book is for sale. In fact, you can even start running ads for your book when it's up for pre-order, although you won't always see as much return on investment prior to release.

As excited as you may be to get started with your ads, there are times when it may be too early to run an ad. Sometimes people won't read a book by an author they don't know, if it doesn't have any book reviews. If your book only has a handful of reviews, that's a tell-tale sign that a book is either not being read or isn't popular, which leads a potential reader to ask, "Why aren't other people reading and reviewing the book?" A lack of reviews can be a turn-off, especially if the only reviews there are 5-star reviews, which is a sign of a book that has only been reviewed by family. It's a cruel reality, but books with a mixed set of reviews (including those cringe-worthy one-star reviews) mark a book as more legitimate. This means that you may want to try to hold off doing paid advertisements until after the book has a handful of reviews.

Experimenting With Ads

When it comes to paid ads, there's no clear right or wrong way to set-up an ad. I'm going to try my best to describe the process for you, but always know you'll get the best results when you take the time to learn the platform, how it works, and what you can do to get the most out of your investment.

In order to learn what works when marketing books, you need to try different graphics, sales copy and targeting to discover what works best. You won't know what graphic or copy works until you try a few different combinations.

Target your ad so it finds the perfect reader. Craft the ad copy so well that they don't *think* they should buy it, they *must* buy it.

Creating a successful ad is not a "one and done." You create an initial ad or two. Put it out there and see how it performs. Then adjust different factors of your ad until you've maximized the ROI. That's how you create a successful book ad.

CHAPTER 1:
YOUR IDEAL READER

"Even when you are marketing to your entire audience or customer base, you are still simply speaking to a single human at any given time."
– Ann Handley

BEFORE WE CAN start learning how to set up ads to sell books, we need to know who our ideal reader is, because they are the person we're trying to talk to about our books. Our ideal reader is the person who is a *perfect* fit for our book. This is someone who will read the book, love it from start to finish, write a five star review, and then tell all their friends about the book so they'll read it too. Our goal is always to find the ideal reader and tell them that our book exists. If we don't market to our ideal reader, not only are we wasting our time, but we're also selling our book to someone who isn't the right fit. Why is it bad to sell your book to someone who isn't a good fit? Besides the fact that they won't enjoy it, they could also leave a one-star review because it "wasn't their cup of tea."

While it's always a dream that everyone will love your book, it's not realistic. No one loves every book they read. If your goal is to sell your book to *everyone*, whether they hate it or not, then go ahead and risk negative feedback. But if you'd like to market your book to readers who will love and cherish your book, then it's time to identify your ideal reader.

When you market to your ideal reader you'll notice a higher ROI because you're not wasting your efforts trying to convince an uninterested reader to pick up your book. Plus, if you market to people who will love your book, you don't need to convince them to buy it. Your only job is to make sure they know the book exists.

How to Discover Your Ideal Reader

We're going to make a profile of your ideal reader, similar to what we do when we're drafting a novel and make a profile of our characters so we know who they are. If you'd like, name your ideal reader and draw a little sketch of what they look like, create a cartoon avatar, or find some inspiration on

Pinterest. This last part isn't a necessary step in the process, but if you find it helps, then go for it!

What Genre Do They Read?

The first thing you need to do is figure out what genres your ideal reader likes. Start off with some general genres like fantasy, thriller, and dystopian. If someone read your story and wanted to rate it as their all-time favorite book, what are their favorite genres? What is their favorite parts of that genre that makes them love it so much? If you've already written your book, what genre is it and what aspects of it make it a perfect fit for that reader?

Once you've written down the general genre, think really specific like Young Adult Dark Fantasy. You'll also want to write down the genres that your ideal reader *doesn't* like. What's something that could turn your ideal reader away from picking up your book? Writing all this down will give you a better idea of who you want to sell your book to and how you can make a connection with them, as well as where you're going to find them.

What Other Authors Do They Read?

Now that you know what genres your ideal reader does and does not like, it's time to think about what authors they like. What authors will your reader read no matter what the book is about? What are other authors in this industry doing correctly? How are they connecting with their readers?

Try to think not only in terms of the big-name authors, but also lesser-known or indie authors. Make sure these authors reflect the genres of your ideal reader, and if they don't, adjust your selection of authors.

How Would They Describe Your Book to a Friend?

This is the fun part. Imagine your ideal reader just finished reading your book and they loved it. Five-star rating! They're going out to lunch with their best friend who also loves to read and they can't wait to talk about your book. How would they describe it? Write down a few words and phrases. Don't be afraid to get creative! Remember, this is supposed to be a fun exercise and there are no wrong answers. You're the only person who will see this profile sheet of your ideal reader, so let your imagination soar! Let your ideal reader describe your book like it's a story they'll read over and over again. Now is not the time to be humble!

As you write out a few phrases of how your ideal reader would describe your novel, they might be different from how you normally would have pitched your novel. This is because sometimes, as the author of your own book, you get too involved in the pitching and marketing process to properly describe your story. When someone is genuinely excited about your book, they'll describe what their favorite parts are, not the issues that stuck out to them.

Sometimes for this part of the exercise, it may be a good idea to turn to your critique partner and beta readers and ask them what they loved about your book. Don't ask to them to describe the book, just ask what they liked about it. Was it a scene, an emotion, a character? Those are the things you want to write down because they will help you find your ideal reader and learn how to market to them.

What Is Their Demographic?

Now that you know your ideal reader a little better, it's time to get even more specific. Write down your ideal reader's demographic. I already know what you're thinking: "My book is perfect for everyone!" It's not. Sure, sometimes people who don't fit into your category of "ideal reader" will love your book, but that doesn't mean that will always be the case. When you first started writing your book, what type of people did you imagine reading it? For example, if you write young adult fantasy, the answer might be high school girls.

To find the demographic of your ideal reader, you'll need to start by identifying their age range and gender.

Where is Your Ideal Reader Hiding?

Do you feel like you know your readers yet? Let's take things a little bit further. Ask yourself these questions about your ideal reader:

- What are their hobbies outside of reading?

- What websites or online influencers do they follow?
- Where do they normally discover the next book they'll read? Book club? The library? Goodreads? Facebook?
- Are they on social media?
- What's their favorite social media platform?

Having all this information may seem a little overboard right now, but this information is the most important part. This information reveals where you can find your ideal reader and gives you an idea of where you need to be so your book can be discovered. Does your ideal reader love books featured on a specific blog? If the answer is yes, find out how you can get your book featured on that blog.

Finding Your Readers' Problem & Solution

For non-fiction, there is a certain type of psychology that goes into marketing a book. Because with non-fiction, especially how-to non-fiction, you're essentially selling a solution to a problem your ideal reader is having. How can your book solve their problems? Here are some questions you need to ask yourself about your ideal reader:

- What is their ultimate goal?
- What is a struggle that's holding them back?
- What do they seek to learn or discover?
- What will your book solve for them?

Tap into your ideal reader's emotions and see what you can find.

Comparative Titles

Have you made a list of comparative titles for your book before? If not, now is the time. Comparative titles, also known as comp titles, are other books in your genre or market that are similar to yours. They are the books you look at when you want to compare marketing techniques or the books you use to describe similarities to your own story. *If you're a fan of The Hunger Games, then you'll love...*

Just like discovering your ideal reader, making a list of your book's comp titles is imperative to knowing how to market your novel. Try to make a list of at least ten novels that are similar to your book in terms of:

- Genre
- Audience
- Subject/theme

When you're writing down your comp titles, make sure to also write down the authors of the books. Hopefully you'll notice a pattern in your comp titles. Do you have a lot of the same authors or genre?

This will solidify that you're marketing your novel to the correct audience. If your comp titles are a bit all over the place in theme or genre, try to better nail down what you think your book is about. If you're struggling with this step, ask your beta readers or critique partner to give some ideas for comp titles.

Your Completed Profile

Have your ideal reader profile filled out? Hold onto it, because you'll use it when creating paid ads, or whenever you do any type of marketing. When you need a comparative title for your book, look at your ideal reader profile. Or if you want to know where to put ads for your book, look at the profile to find out if you're marketing in a space where you know your readers are present. As I work through this book, you'll hear me refer back to your ideal reader often, because again, you don't want to waste your time and money on someone who won't like your book. Always market your book as if you're targeting these readers and not the masses.

Your ideal reader profile is something you'll want to create for every book you write because they will change and shift for each individual book. Keep it on hand whenever you're creating any promotion and think of how you can target your ad in a way that it is aimed directly at your ideal reader.

If you'd like a printable of the ideal reader profile, you can download it for free when you subscribe to my newsletter:

http://bit.ly/MandisNews

BETHANY'S TIPS:

If you're like me, you've heard book marketers talk about your ideal reader before, but it's always super vague and hard to nail down. I really appreciate Mandi's focus on getting specific, because it helps you picture that person sitting down in front of the Amazon webpage clicking, "Add to Cart."

Knowing that changes everything.

If I know my reader well, then I can guess what they're typing into the search bar, which helps me get my book in front of them with the right keywords, and just as importantly, it helps me know how to create ads they'll be drawn to.

Knowing your ideal reader is all about reverse engineering the marketing process, starting with your end goal and working your way backward.

Most authors keep their marketing generic because they want to reach the widest audience possible, but what they don't realize is that this actually alienates people more than it draws them in. One of the biggest tips I always hear when it comes to knowing your ideal reader, is that the more specific you can be, the better.

CHAPTER 2:
CREATING GRAPHICS & SALES COPY

"Make it simple. Make it memorable.

Make it inviting to look at"

– Leo Bur

FOR ALMOST ALL the promotion methods in this book you'll need graphics and/or sales copy. It's easy enough to create a graphic on your own and write a quick sentence about why people should buy your book, but how will you know if it will translate into sales?

For most authors, mastering the art of creating successful graphics and sales copy will take time and practice. In this chapter, I'm going to walk you through the steps of creating professional and eye-catching graphics for your book, as well as writing sales copy that will have people thinking, "Oh! I need to read this book!"

Sometimes you'll need only sales copy or only a graphic. Then other times you might need both. Here are a few examples of the type of content you'll need depending on the type of ad you want to create:

Amazon Ad: sales copy only

Facebook Ad: graphic & sales copy

Newsletter Feature/Ad: graphic only

There are dozens of other situations where you might be creating an ad, but the goal is to create a graphic and/or sales copy about your book that is so good that people want to click and buy immediatley. If you're doing an ad on Amazon, you only have one sentence to convince people they need to buy your book. On the other hand, if you want to feature your book in a newsletter, you might only have a 400 x 300 pixel space to tell people why they need to buy your book.

Because ads are so short, we have minimal space to convince someone to read our book, so we have to take extra care when crafting them. So let's start with some fundamentals to creating sales copy.

Text That Sells

The text you have in your design should be short and sweet, since most ads are small. You have to make sure whatever text you put in your design can be read if the ad was shrunk down. Also, if you do an ad through Facebook (which we'll talk about in Chapter Six), you can't have text in your graphic take up more than 20% of the image. Whatever text you do have, it has to be short, sweet, and sell that book.

Here are some great examples of the kind of text you can put in your ad:

- Quotes from reviews: "I couldn't put it down! – name" or "What readers are saying…"
- Credentials: "Best selling author of ____"
- A one-sentence pitch of the book: "Dark contemporary meets medical thriller in this story about a fight for a cure, despite what may be right or wrong."
- Comp-titles: "If you loved ____ than you'll love ____."

- Discounts: "Available for $1.99 for limited time!"
- Teaser content like an excerpt: "Start reading _____ for free!"

What Is Good Design?

When it comes to graphic design, there are some rules to follow. These rules can be broken, but they should only be broken after they have first been mastered. Below I have six graphic design concepts that you should always keep in mind when creating any sort of graphic to promote your book that will make your ads look clean and professional:

1. **Balance** - When designing, everything should be balanced, whether that balance is symmetrical or asymmetrical. If you create a graphic where half the space is taken up by your book cover, the over

half of the graphic needs to have *something*, whether that be another graphic or text.

2. **Color** – Color is a language all its own. When it comes to designing something simple like a graphic for your book, choose about three colors to work with, that way the graphic isn't too busy. Choose colors that complement each other, rather than colors that clash. Colors that clash that are too close in tone and look muddled when they're next to each other. Complementary colors have contrast, so that when they're next to each other they pop and stand out. If you want a fool-proof way to choose colors, try Adobe's color tool to choose colors that complement each other, rather than contrast: <https://color.adobe.com/create>

When I see book graphics gone wrong, it's usually because the colors are too bold, or there are too many colors. Pick colors that match your book's cover rather than colors that will take attention away from your book cover. After all, the book's cover is half the sales pitch.

3. **Contrast** - Make your text readable by using contrast! I can't tell you how many times I've seen graphics where the text didn't have enough contrast from the background, which made it blend in and difficult to read. If you design something and can't read it easily from far away or if the text gets lost in a busy background, create more contrast by choosing different colors or having a simple background. No matter what, your ad must be easy to read.

4. **Hierarchy** - Create a hierarchy of information. What is the most important thing in your graphic? Whatever is the biggest or boldest is what the eye will go to first, which is how you create a hierarchy of information. If you're an indie author, the most important part won't be your name. It will probably be a one-liner about your book or a quote from a review. On the other hand, the most important part of the graphic for a New York Times Best Seller, for example, would be the author's name.

5. **Text** - A good rule of thumb is to never use more than three types of text in a design. Keep it simple and create variation in your text by using italics and bold. Try to stay away from decorative fonts because it will make text unreadable from far away.

6. **Simplicity** - My final tip will always be to keep your design simple. Often someone who isn't familiar with graphic design will overcompensate and do too much in a design, which can be overwhelming and distracting. Less is always more. Overcomplicated designs can look unprofessional, which might make the reader will assume your book may be the same way.

Where to Create Your Design

By now, I'm sure you're wondering where you'll go to actually design your graphic. I kindly ask that you stay away from Word, or dare I say, PowerPoint. There are plenty of free and easy to use graphic design tools out there at your disposal.

One of my favorites is Book Brush. Book Brush is designed for creating book ads and graphics. There are templates that you can choose from, or you can start from scratch and create your own.

They provide everything you'll need from a 3D cover generator, to a variety of buttons you can add into your design. Book Brush also has a Facebook group you can join where authors are welcome to post their designs and get feedback. I'm a member of the group, so if you share your work you may even get feedback from me one day!

As of right now, Book Brush's free plan gives you three designs a month, but their paid plan is reasonably priced and has unlimited designs a month and also a bigger variety of templates.

Here are some other great tools that you can use to design ads, as well as a very simple break-down of what they can do:

- Canva
    - Free and paid options

- o Create graphics using templates, with text, stickers and more
- PicMonkey
    - o Free and paid options
    - o Edit photos and add stickers
- Adobe Spark
    - o Free and paid options
    - o Create graphics using templates
- Adobe Photoshop
    - o Paid only option
    - o Create just about anything

What Should Go In a Book Ad Design?

There are so many different ways you can go about designing a graphic that you'll use to sell your book, but when it comes down to it, a good ad usually contains four things:

1. The book cover
2. Text that sells
3. A link to purchase the book
4. A background

The Book Cover

There are a few different ways you can incorporate your book cover into your design. The simplest way would be to just paste the JPEG of the cover into the design. If you want to step things up a bit, you can also create a 3D-rendering of book.

If you'd like a free resource to create 3D-rendering of your book, fellow author, Derek Murphy, created a tool accessible to everyone, which you can find here:

www.diybookcovers.com/3Dmockups/

Simply upload your cover, choose the type of 3D you want, and follow the steps on the website. When you download the finished 3D rendering, I recommend you choose to download it as a PNG file so the background will be transparent and you can place the cover anywhere without having to worry about a white background.

A Link to Purchase the Book

This part isn't necessary, but often the graphic you create is all you have to sell your book. For example, if you have an ad in a newsletter, you're usually only allowed to have a graphic and no sales copy. This isn't always the case, but you will find a lot of times when you're advertising your book, the only thing you'll have to sell it will be the graphic you create. In this case, your graphic will need to be "clickable" to remind anyone that comes across the ad that if they're interested in the book, they should click on the graphic.

To do this, you'll have to add something that looks like a button into your ad. You can create buttons for your graphic easily using many tools, like Book Brush, Canva, or even Photoshop. Your button could say whatever you'd like. When I create buttons, I like to say "Start Reading" or "Learn More," because "Buy Now" is blunt and might turn people away.

A Background

The background should be the easiest part of your design, but sometimes this is what authors struggle with most because they overthink it. Choose a simple background, something that won't take away from the book. Remember, this is all about hierarchy of information. The background is the least important part of the ad, so it shouldn't even be noticed. It should just blend in with the rest of the design. If your background is confetti, for example, not only will it draw away from the book cover, but it will also cause the text to get lost and become unreadable. If you choose to have an image in your background because it fits the mood of the books, you can fade the image out so the focus is still on the book and the text.

Sales Copy That Sells

Creating graphics can be fun! But now that you've learned how to create a stunning graphic to sell your book, it's time to talk about sales copy that goes with your graphic. Authors have a gift to write thousands of words for our stories, but when it comes to summing it all up into just one sentence, it suddenly feels impossible. If you're creating an Amazon ad, the only thing you have to sell your novel is your sales copy and the cover of your book.

If you're creating a Facebook ad, you'll have a graphic to go with your sales copy, but at the end of the day your sales copy needs to wow your audience.

Why should people read your book? That's ultimately what people need to know.

The sales copy will be the same type of text you put in your graphics: review quotes, credentials, one-sentence pitch, comp titles, discounts, and teasers. The difference here is, you have more space to say what you need to sell your book. And by more room, I mean you might be able to fit an extra sentence. Sales copy should not be long. It will be one, maybe two sentences trying to tell someone why your book is a perfect fit for them. If you can't sell someone after the second sentence, they probably aren't going to read the third sentence.

Whatever you use as sales copy, make sure it's different from whatever you used as text so you aren't being repetitive. One of the hardest types of sales copy to write can be the one-sentence pitch, so let's dive deeper.

The One-Sentence Pitch

My favorite type of ad copy is the one-sentence pitch. Essentially, it's your elevator pitch. You only have a minute or two to tell someone what your book is about and why they'd want to read it. So how do you do that in just one sentence? Throw your potential readers right into the action. What is at stake and what's this book really about?

"Dark contemporary meets medical thriller in this story about a fight for a cure despite what may be right or wrong."

This is one version of sales copy I used for thriller novel, *She's Not Here*. And yes, I have multiple ways I pitch my books depending on the platform and which niche of my audience I'm talking to. You should always think of your audience when you're pitching your novel. This is why it's so important to fill out your ideal reader profile, so you know who you're talking to and what, specifically, about your book, has them interested. For the sales copy of *She's Not Here*, I put the genre of the book front and center, as well as what's at stake, because that's the selling point of the novel.

What about your story makes it so intereFsting? Whatever the hook is for your story, craft it into one sentence, so when your target reader comes across it, they feel like they have to buy the book so they can find out what happens.

When coming up with a way to sell your book and make it stand out, ask yourself, "What makes my book different?"

BETHANY'S TIPS:

Like Mandi said, when it comes to those hundred words (or less) in your ad, the writing can suddenly feel impossible.

Graphics and sales copy can both be overwhelming, especially to a new author. My biggest tip is to research other author's ads, before you start creating your own. Pay attention to ads by successful authors as well as ads for books in the same genre as your story. Take notes on different writing styles, different calls to action, and different color schemes. Research how ads appear on different sites, such as Amazon, Barnes & Noble, Facebook, BookBub, Goodreads, and anywhere else you see books being promoted.

Most importantly, take notes on which advertising strategies work best on you. Because while we never want to copy another author's story, there's nothing wrong with imitating another author's marketing style (or even better, merging multiple marketing styles together to form your own).

When I first started out, I pulled bits and pieces of sales copy from other authors I admired. This is how I learned what worked for me and what didn't, as well as which types of graphics and sales copy I most enjoyed using myself.

For example, if you want to copy a call to action word for word, such as, "Click to read more," you can. As you get comfortable, you can start tweaking these marketing phrases into something more unique that reflects your personality, like changing that button to say, "You Know You Want to Read More!"

I know it's overwhelming when you first start out, so just remember, good marketing is a lot of trial and error. Try different styles, allow yourself errors, and keep going until you find what works!

CHAPTER 3:
NEWSLETTER SWAPS & FEATURES

"Alone we can do so little;

together we can do so much."

– Helen Keller

IN BOOK TWO of this series, *Grow Your Author Platform*, we talked about how important email lists are because they give you direct access to your followers. You don't have to worry about social media algorithms changing. You just have to worry about your emails being interesting enough that people stay subscribed and open the emails.

The same goes for other people's email lists. That is what this chapter is going to be all about: how to take advantage of email lists cultivated by others to reach a new set of readers. This can be done by connecting with fellow authors and book community influencers.

Free Newsletter Swaps

What is a newsletter swap? This is when two (or more) authors agree to feature the other(s) in their newsletter. You will get exposure to a new audience and neither of you have to pay to do it. If you don't have a newsletter yet, or you want help growing yours, be sure to read book two in *Marketing for Authors: Grow Your Author Platform.*

What Do You Need for a Newsletter Swap?

Newsletter swaps are usually setup similar to an ad, in that you create some graphics with the book's cover on it and maybe include your blurb. Because this is an author-run ad so to speak, the owner of the newsletter can feature you however they'd like. It can look like an ad, like we talked about above, or it could be a mini interview of some sort, or anything in-between.

When you swap with someone, you can always brainstorm how to do the feature, and make sure that however they feature you, that you do the same for them. You get what you give, so always be generous in the writing community. If you aren't sure what the person you're swapping with needs from you in terms of graphics and sales copy, ask them for examples of swaps they've run in the past to get ideas.

Finding Someone to Swap With

Okay, that sounds great and all, but what if you don't know a lot of other authors? Or maybe the ones you do know either write in a different genre or you've already done a newsletter swap with them. The good news is that there is an endless supply of authors willing to do newsletter swaps, you just need to find them.

I first heard of newsletter swaps from the 20Booksto50K Facebook group. This is a group of authors that formed based off the idea that in order to make it as a full-time author and make $50,000 a year, you typically need to have 20 books for sale.

This concept was created by Michael Anderle, and while 20 books isn't a one-size-fits-all number for every writer, it's a group full of so much valuable information. Even if you don't agree with the concept or aren't looking for someone for a newsletter swap, I still suggest that you join the group to learn as much as you can. Just make sure to read the group guidelines before posting anything because you could be removed and blocked from the group without warning if you don't follow the guidelines.

When it comes to finding someone to do a newsletter swap in a Facebook Group like this, it's pretty simple: ask. Make a post in the group with following information:

- What genre is your book that you want to feature?

- What genre(s) do your newsletter readers enjoy?
- How large is your newsletter?
- When did you want to do the newsletter swap?

If you're lucky, you'll get a few responses. You can also keep an eye out for posts from other authors looking to do a newsletter swap.

Facebook Groups Dedicated to Author Newsletter Swaps:

- Author Newsletter Share and Swap
- Romance Authors Newsletter Swap
- Author Newsletter Swap and Cross Promo

These are some of the most popular newsletter groups I've found on Facebook, but you can find smaller niche groups by going to Facebook and searching, "Author Newsletter," and then filtering Facebook's search option to groups.

As always, be sure to read the group's guidelines before you start posting. It's very easy to accidentally become spammy, and many group admins will delete you if they feel you aren't adding to the community.

Not a huge fan of Facebook? Here are a few other places you can find authors to do newsletter swaps:

- StoryOrigin
- BookBoast
- AXP Newsletter Swap Club
- Goodreads Groups
- Reddit

StoryOrigin is one of my new favorites that I recently discovered and it's something I suggest all authors check out because it's more than just a newsletter swap platform. StoryOrigin is a community of authors that band together to cross-promote their books to get more reviews, increase sales or pages reads, and build email lists. The platform handles all the harder "tech" side of things so authors can spend more time writing and working together. So far the platform allows you to send advanced reader copies to readers, find newsletter swaps, and do joint giveaways with other authors. The site is constantly growing and getting new features, so I suggest you check it out!

BookBoast and AXP Newsletter Swap Club are similar platforms, that I also recommend and will give similar results. For Goodreads and Reddit, you'll have to find an author newsletter swap thread/forum on the website, which are usually sectioned off by genre.

How to Collect Information Using Google Forms

If you decide to do a newsletter swap, you'll need to collect information from another author, maybe a lot of authors! Do yourself a favor and use a Google Form to collect all the info you'll need. The best part? Google Forms are free and user-friendly!

Let's imagine you're in a Facebook newsletter swap group and you want to see if some authors want to participate in a swap with you. A great way to collect a lot of information from multiple authors is to create a post in the group saying you're looking for people to feature in your newsletter, along with a link to a Google Form you created to collect everyone's information.

Let's break down what your Google Form should contain:

1. Information about your newsletter & book. At the top of your form, you'll be able to put all the information the other author will want to know, such as:
   - Number of newsletter subscribers you have
   - Genre of your book
   - Your book's summary
   - A link to your book on Amazon

2. Information for the other author to fill out:
   - Their name/pen name
   - Email
   - Book's genre
   - Book's description
   - Link to book on Amazon
   - Size of their newsletter
   - Contact info

Once authors fill out the form you can look through the results, decide who will be a good fit for your newsletter, and contact them to schedule your swap.

You can also message an author directly. If you like an author's book and you feel your book would be a good match for that author's audience as well, reach out and ask if they'd be interested in doing a newsletter swap. Before you ask, do your research and subscribe to their newsletter. See if they ever feature books by other authors. If they don't, then know that they might not be interested in doing a swap.

When contacting other authors, it's always best to be professional and email them, rather than reaching out in messages on social media. When you email, be sure to include information about yourself, how many subscribers your newsletter has, as well as a description of your book. This will give the other author enough information to decide whether or not they may be interested in working with you. As someone who gets contacted on a regular basis by other authors, there is nothing more frustrating than getting contacted by an author who just tells me they wrote a book, wants me to feature their book, but doesn't tell me anything *about* the book.

Before You Agree to a Swap

It's time to talk about our ideal reader! If you're thinking of doing a newsletter swap with someone, ask yourself if this is a newsletter your ideal reader would be subscribed to. If the answer is no, then you might want to skip that newsletter.

Quality is Everything

Don't do a newsletter swap with everyone under the sun. Remember, you're putting the quality of your newsletter on the line. If your own newsletters are nothing but newsletter swaps just so your book can be featured in other newsletters, your emails will start to look like spam in someone else's inbox.

Chose books to feature that you think your subscribers would genuinely enjoy and meet the same standards your book does. Not every indie book published is quality and you reserve the right to use your newsletter to feature what you consider quality books. This is your reputation on the line. It only takes one click for someone to decide they no longer find your newsletter useful and unsubscribe.

If you decide you need to turn down someone's offer for a newsletter feature, simply tell them that you feel their book may not be a good fit for your subscribers. And if you aren't willing to feature someone in your newsletter, don't assume they'll still be willing to feature you in theirs. Newsletter swaps are all about give and take.

Give Your Information All At Once

Once you schedule a swap with another author and have discussed what you need to send to them (links, graphic, sales copy, etc.) send it all at once. Put it all in one email, or attach it to the email as a ZIP folder, or upload everything into one folder on DropBox or Google Drive. Make the collaboration with the other author as easy as possible so that author will want to work with you again in the future.

The Downside to Free Newsletter Feature Swaps

Free marketing is great! But free marketing isn't always quality marketing. Sometimes you can find an author with thousands of subscribers, but those email lists can be hard to come by. And if you are able to find them, it's likely hard to get a feature because they're selective. They could easily have a long list of authors willing to do newsletter features, but only a handful will meet their standards.

More often you'll find a newsletter with a handful of subscribers. It's up to you to decide whether you want to do these smaller features. On the bright side, it won't hurt you to do them. There's still a possibility that you'll find new readers. At the worst, you'll just waste time arranging the newsletter feature.

Do keep in mind that sometimes the smaller newsletters are full of loyal subscribers, while email lists with a large amount of followers can sometimes be impersonal and full of inactive subscribers. That's not always the case, but it's something to keep in mind when doing swaps with authors who have smaller numbers. Don't turn down a newsletter swap just because the other person has a smaller list than you.

Paid Newsletter Features

Now I wish I could say all newsletter swaps were free. The larger a newsletter gets, the more your odds of needing to pay for a feature will increase. If you're paying to have your book featured, then the newsletter should have a significantly larger following.

A rule of thumb is that you shouldn't have to pay to have your book featured in another author's newsletter. The "price" should be the swap. Now, just because that's the unspoken etiquette, doesn't mean you won't come across it. I'm sure there are many authors out there who have large email lists and charge for a feature.

This is a personal choice, and one I don't recommend doing yourself, mostly because this goes against the "give and take" concept in the writing community. If you're only "taking" you're defeating the purpose of the swap. Paid features also make the integrity of your newsletter questionable. Is the author of the newsletter still being selective of what they feature, or will they feature anything as long as the fee is paid?

Your newsletter is valuable, and you deserve to be selective about what you feature. Having "ad space" blurs the lines between quality content and spam. Your newsletter subscribers trust you, so keep that trust by only featuring books you think your audience would genuinely enjoy.

Should You Pay For a Newsletter Feature?

Paying to feature your book on an author's newsletter is a personal choice. As someone who's considered paying to feature my book, but hasn't done it, I have yet to find an author who charges a price that reflects the size and quality of their email list. You have to keep in mind that in an average email list only 60% will open the email. And out of those who open it, maybe another 3% will click your link, and *maybe* buy your book.

Let's say someone has a newsletter with 5,000 subscribers and they charge $100 for ad space. If the open rate, which is the percentage of people that open the email, is 60%, then 3,000 are actually opening the email. Of those 3,000 people, only 3% of them (or roughly 90 people) may click the link. Will all 90 people buy the book? Probably not. In fact, I'd guess maybe 20% will buy it, which is just 18 people. Which means that out of the 5,000 subscribers, only 18 people bought the book. If you make about $2 a book, then you just made $36, but you spent $100 on the ad. Not worth it.

Now these percentages are not set in stone or standard numbers. Each newsletter will have different open-rates and click-through rates (i.e. the percentage of people that click a link in an email). Some authors will tell you what their rates are, but many won't. An open-rate of 60% is considered a very healthy number for a newsletter.

If you can find an author with a paid newsletter feature at the right price, the odds of someone buying your book reading an author's newsletter versus a company's newsletter is slightly better. When you're the only book featured in an author's newsletter, the subscribers may see your book as a personal recommendation. Their favorite author liked your book, so they'll probably like it too. When it comes to doing paid author newsletter features, just make sure you do your research. Does the audience of the newsletter fit the genre of your book? How will your book be featured and how prominent will the feature be? How was the experience of past authors who have had their book featured?

Tracking Your Information & ROI

Newsletter swaps are low-tech compared to other types of marketing we'll discuss in this book, so it can be harder to know the ROI, but it is possible! One way you can collect data on how your ad performed in the newsletter swap is to use a Bit.ly link. Bit.ly is useful for shortening URLs, but it also tracks the number of clicks on that link.

Bit.ly accounts are free to create and it's a resource I can't brag about enough! When you do a newsletter swap, copy and paste your Amazon link into Bit.ly and give the shortened link to the author you're swapping with. When the newsletter goes out, you'll be able to go into your Bit.ly account and see how many people clicked on your book from that newsletter alone. When you create your Bit.ly links, be sure to label/name them so you know where the clicks are coming from.

If you decide you love doing newsletter swaps, you can start scheduling some out for months at a time. Create a spreadsheet where you can track dates, sales, and anything else you don't want to lose track of!

BETHANY'S TIPS:

When a newsletter is smaller, those subscribers can often be "super fans" which means they're more devoted to that author and more willing to listen to a recommendation. Don't dismiss a smaller newsletter as not worth your time, when in fact, it could potentially sell just as many or even more books! This step is definitely one that I wish I did more often, considering the only investment in most cases is time!

My advice would be to start with authors you know personally. There could be a bit of a learning curve, but if you're working with friends when you first start out, they'll help you through any surprises and pretty soon you'll be a pro. Not everyone enjoys newsletter swaps, and as Mandi pointed out, most author's want to avoid doing them too often to prevent sounding spammy, so try to avoid pressuring another author into doing a swap. Instead offer it to them as a potential opportunity and let them decide if it's a good fit for them.

Last, but not least, make sure you're always investing time into the quality of your own newsletter. Maybe even consider promoting some books that you love without any strings attached. That way, if another author is interested in a swap with you, you can show them how you've promoted other authors in the past.

CHAPTER 4:
EBOOK PROMOTION SITES

"You can't expect to just write and have visitors come to you – that's too passive."

– Anita Campbell

WE'VE TALKED ABOUT how to get your book featured in an author newsletter, but what about getting your book featured by book promotion companies with thousands of newsletter subscribers, each one focusing on a certain genre? It's an ideal book promotion opportunity. A book company's newsletter means directly targeting potentially thousands of readers who love fantasy, for example. In this scenario, if you have your fantasy book featured in a book company's newsletter, it means directly targeting thousands of readers that love fantasy and discovering new authors.

Book companies often form multiple lists of email subscribers based on genre. If someone is interested in thriller novels, they can subscribe to that specific list. If someone likes contemporary, they'll subscribe to that newsletter, and so on. Book company newsletters can be powerful, because readers subscribe to those newsletters specifically to discover new books in their favorite genre.

Submit Your Book to BookBub

The most common book newsletter is BookBub. BookBub is a company dedicated to creating lists of ebook sales and recommendations to their subscribers, whether those books are best-sellers or hidden gems. Readers can choose to subscribe to a certain genre's email list and they'll get emails alerting them of sales and free ebooks. BookBub has thousands of subscribers on each of their lists and is a gold mine if you're able to squeeze into a spot on their newsletter. Of course, you have to pay for your spot, but it's well worth it.

BookBub is very transparent with the size of their newsletters and how many downloads authors can expect. In fact, they have an entire page on their website to give you an idea of how many books you might sell:

https://www.bookbub.com/partners/pricing

Let's take crime novels for example. As of right now, their crime novels email list has almost four million subscribers. If you're running a sale on your ebook so it's $0.99, you'll pay about $1,138 dollars for the BookBub feature, but you can expect about 3,600 downloads of your book. This means if you're making 70% off each ebook, you're making $2,494.80, which means after subtracting what you paid for the ad you're left with $1,356.80. Now that's what we call return on investment! Again, these are hypothetical numbers, but you get the idea!

This email list works because these readers are eager to find their next book. They're ready to buy. That's why they subscribed! They're also looking for a good deal. Readers will be more likely to buy an ebook that costs $0.99 from an author they've never heard of than spend $9.99 on a paperback. This is why BookBub, as well as many other book promotion websites, focus on ebooks, because there is low risk factor if the readers don't like the book.

The catch is that it's difficult to get in a BookBub newsletter. Because they're so popular, thousands of authors apply to have their book featured. BookBub tends to be pretty selective with what books they feature because they want quality content in their newsletters. One of their main deciding factors is how many reviews the book has. If your book doesn't have at least 30 reviews then assume that you won't be considered. Even if you do have enough reviews, you're not always given a spot.

Requirements to Have Your Book Listed on BookBub:

- Free or discounted by at least 50%—they only feature books with great sale prices.

- Best deal possible—if you just ran a sale to have your book as a free download, but you're trying to have it listed in BookBub during your 50% off sale, they won't list it in their newsletter until at least 90 days have passed since the last sale.
- Error free—if your book has typos and errors, they won't consider you.
- Limited Time—the offer that you have for your book should be for a set period of time; they don't feature books that are always available at a low price.
- Full length books—novels, novellas, and short story collections must be at least 100 pages
- Widely available—your book must be for sale through at least one large US or UK retailer
- Spread out features—they will only feature a book once every 6 months, and they will only feature the same author once every 30 days.

Submit Your Book to Other Bookish Companies

While this may be discouraging, know that BookBub is not the only company of its kind that creates email lists like this. Here's a list of websites similar to BookBub: *(see resources section for links)*

- Awesomegang
- Book Cave
- BookSends
- Book Sliced
- Bookperk
- Books Butterfly
- eBook Soda
- eReader News Today
- FreeBooksy
- Kindle Nation Daily
- Genre Pulse
- GoodKindles

- Reading Deals
- Robin Reads
- The Fussy Librarian

This list could go on and on. In fact, more sites like this are created every day. A great way to discover them is to talk to other indie authors and ask them where they promote their books and which they think are the best. Some sites are better than others though, because anyone can create a book email list and charge to have your book featured. As you know from the last chapter, just because an email list has thousands of subscribers that doesn't mean it has great open rates or clicks. See if you can find other indie authors and get their personal recommendations or look online for reviews before you try a paid promotion on a site you've never heard of before.

Submit Your Book to Free Book Features

Up until this point, I've only mentioned sites that charge to have your book featured. But there are also book promotion websites/newsletters that will promote your book for free. The only thing you have to invest is your time in discovering the websites and submitting your book.

Unfortunately, because these sites are free, they often come and go. Whoever runs the email list might lose their passion, or funds grow tight, or really anything could happen because the list isn't generating the same type of income as those that charge authors for features. That said, it's still something you can take advantage of while they're going strong.

Some of the sites below are newsletters, some are listings from an online directory, and some of them will tweet about your book: *(see resources section for links)*

- Author Marketing Club
- Babs Book Bistro
- Bargin Booksy
- BookCircleOnline
- Book Raid
- E Reader Girl
- Daily Bookworm
- Digital Book Today
- Indie Author News
- Inkitt
- Pretty Hot Books

A lot of these sites will have options for free advertising or paid advertising. I'd recommend trying out the free version first and if you notice a rise in sales or downloads, you could upgrade yourself to the paid version to get even more exposure for your book.

Submitting to all these websites can take time, but if you aren't comfortable with setting up ads or don't have a large author platform, these types of websites can be the perfect way to boost your sales without much thought. While it takes time to submit to all the websites, it doesn't require the same knowledge and skill that it would if you wanted to set up an ad for Facebook or Amazon.

BETHANY'S TIPS:

Which type of advertising sounds more helpful for you and your platform? Submitting to ebook promotion sites could honestly end up being a more expensive option, but it could also free you up to get back to writing. You can stop stressing over social media, creating ads yourself, and figuring it out because someone else will take care of it for you. Some of you might not care either way, but others will love that option and feel so relieved!

I'd encourage you to set aside fifteen minutes to research one or more of the companies we've mentioned, review their current pricing and guidelines, and see if it sounds like a good fit for you.

You may decide that while an ebook promo site isn't right for your book at the moment, it might be perfect later on down the road. Or, you might feel that it's too late for your current book that's been out for a year or two, but you can make a note to do this for your next book release.

In my opinion, newsletter swaps and ebook website promo both tend to be more effective when a book is newer—especially right around a book release—because they build up hype for your book, whereas Facebook and Amazon ads can work more long term and be more helpful even after the hype has died down.

CHAPTER 5:
GOODREADS GIVEAWAYS

"If you're not making mistakes, you're probably not experimenting enough."

-Noah Kagan

GOODREADS IS FACEBOOK for book nerds. Users can create digital shelves for the books they've read and the books they want to read, plus post status updates as they read a book. You can add friends, participate in groups, and so much more. It's a great place for readers to hang out and discover new books, and it can also be a great place for authors to post about their books and build a following.

There's a lot to be said about creating an author profile on Goodreads, but for today I want to talk in particular about hosting a Goodreads giveaway.

Once upon a time, you could host a giveaway on Goodreads for free, but in November of 2017 they changed giveaways to a paid feature, meaning if an author wants to have their book featured on the giveaway section of the page, there is an associated fee. Goodreads has broken down their giveaway prizes into the following options (as of June 2019):

Standard Package - $199

The lowest priced option you can choose for the Goodreads Giveaway is the standard package which grants you the following features:

- The book is added to someone's to-read list when they apply to the giveaway
- Entrants receive an email notification about the book on release day
- The giveaway shows up in the feed of anyone who enters the giveaway, giving the book more exposure
- Goodreads reminds the winner(s) to review the book

Premium Package - $599

For those who want to extend their exposure and connection with their audience even further,

Goodreads offer a premium package, which has everything the Standard Package has, plus:

Premium listing in the Goodreads Giveaway section, and an email is sent to everyone who doesn't win the giveaway, reminding them about the book, even if the book hasn't been released yet.

What Can Readers Win?

In the past you could only give away paperback or hardcover editions of books, but the new packages allow you to give away ebooks as well, which at least saves you money on shipping books to the winner.

Even better, you can give away up to 100 copies of your book. Why is that a good thing? Because the whole point of a Goodreads Giveaway is to gain exposure and reviews. The more copies of your book that you give away, the more potential readers you may gain. This doesn't mean giving away 100 ebooks will translate to 100 guaranteed reviews, but it does mean potential for reviews. And possibly even reviews on Amazon if you ask them (very nicely) to submit the Goodreads review there as well.

Getting Your Book Reviewed

If you decide to do a Goodreads Giveaway, then make it truly worth your time and money by following up with your winners about writing a review. After your winners are chosen, Goodreads will send you the information of those who won, including a link to their profile page, meaning you can personally message them. As it is, Goodreads will message winners eight weeks after the contest ends, reminding them to review the book, but if you want to add a personalized touch, you can message them yourself as well.

A few rules of etiquette when it comes to messaging your winners:

- Be nice
- Don't be pushy
- Be thankful

If someone wins a free copy of your book, they don't owe you anything. They are not obligated to review the book. Heck, they aren't even obligated to read the book. Someone could win a copy of your book and never read the first page. It happens. Those who are active on Goodreads tend to have *lonnnngggg* to be read piles, meaning a book by an unknown author, free or not, may land at the bottom of their reading list.

Now I'm sure you're asking yourself, "Then why did they enter to win my book?"

Because free books are awesome!

I'm sure there are many people who enter giveaways just because a book sounds mildly interesting. But there are also many who enter giveaways that are so excited to read a free ebook. And how do you make your free ebook stand out and become a priority on their to-read list?

Message them personally.

Let them know you're thankful that they entered the giveaway and that you hope they enjoy this story you've created. Remind them what the book is about in a short sentence. Remind them why they wanted to win the book in the first place! Remind them that if they enjoy the book, the best way to support an author is to write a short review on Amazon and Goodreads. Lastly, let them know your inbox is open. I personally love hearing from readers and what their favorite scenes and characters are, so make sure you let them know it's okay for them to message you with any thoughts or questions.

To sum it up, here is what your message should contain:

- A thank you
- Remind them what the book is about
- Ask them to review on Amazon and Goodreads
- Let them know your inbox is always open

Don't message winners about reviewing more than once. If they message you back, talking about the book, that's great! But don't push them to review the book, especially if you've already asked once. The point of messaging users on Goodreads is to make friends, not to promote yourself as an author. Use Goodreads the way it was meant to be used and it will reward you. If you "spam" your giveaway readers, not only could you lose a review, but they could also skip reading your book entirely.

Is a Goodreads Giveaway Worth It?

I haven't done a Goodreads Giveaway since they started charging, but I did do them before they started charging. Even though I didn't have to pay to host my giveaway, I'll let you know what I got in terms of results so you can get an idea of what to expect.

In 2017, I hosted a giveaway for my debut novel, *Essence*. It got 1,859 entries and many of those people added the book to their TBR shelf (although I didn't make it a requirement to enter). What was cool about this giveaway was that the book had been published for 4 years, so it wasn't getting the sales it used to, but the giveaway gave the book a ton of attention. I can't say whether or not it had a spike in sales because back then I wasn't keeping track (remember, I was 17 when *Essence* came out), but I do know my book was shared widely across Goodreads.

I've also heard that since Goodreads now makes authors pay to host a giveaway, they've made it more valuable, meaning your book should be seen more and you'll receive more entries into your giveaway. I explored the giveaways page and it looks like most giveaways get at least 2,000 to 5,000 entries, sometimes much more, so I'd say that at least seems true!

What you have to remember is that the point of Goodreads Giveaways is not sales, but exposure. It's almost impossible to measure ROI. You're paying $199 or more to give your book away for free. To most authors that may seem crazy, but if you want to quickly get reviews for your book or put your book in the hands of your target readers, hosting a Goodreads Giveaway may be your answer.

If You're Considering Hosting a Giveaway, Ask Yourself Two Things:

1. What's my goal for the giveaway?
   - If your goal is book sales... don't do the giveaway
   - If your goal is exposure... do the giveaway
   - If your goal is book reviews... do the giveaway with 100 ebooks to get the most bang for your buck

2. Are my readers on Goodreads?

Most of Goodreads users are females in the United States between the ages of 18 and 44. Now that doesn't mean there aren't men on the site or people over the age of 45, but the numbers of those users are much smaller and harder to reach. If your audience is part of these smaller demographics, consider skipping Goodreads Giveaways.

BETHANY'S TIPS:

One other question you should consider if you are leaning toward a Goodreads Giveaway is, are you comfortable following up with your readers and asking for reviews? I personally believe that a giveaway, whether on Goodreads or otherwise, is usually not worth an author's time and money, unless they're going to get reviews or exposure out of it.

You could post on social media after a giveaway generally asking anyone who's read the book to review, which can occasionally help remind fans to do so. But to make a giveaway truly worth your investment, it's extremely important to find a kind, non-invasive, non-awkward way of reaching out to the winners one-on-one to say something like, "I'm so excited you won (book title), and hope you're enjoying it! If you're comfortable leaving a short review on Amazon and Goodreads, it would mean the world to me!" You could even let them know you'd promote them and their review as well, which helps them in return.

The more reviews your book has, the more confidence a new reader will have to buy it. More reviews essentially equal more book sales in the long run.

If you're not sure how you feel about asking someone for a review, just imagine yourself in their shoes. Avoid being pushy and focus on being friendly and excited to hear their opinion. The more personal you can be in your conversation with someone when you ask them to review (i.e. one-on-one versus in a group text or message), the more likely they will be to review.

CHAPTER 6:
FACEBOOK ADS

"The best Facebook ads look and feel as relevant and timely in your News Feed as the posts you see from your friends."

– Mari Smith

FACEBOOK ADS HAVE changed and shifted over the years and I'm sure they'll continue to do so. As an author, creating ads on Facebook can be an easy way to target your ideal reader like we talked about in chapter one. People set up their Facebook feed to see the content they enjoy. When you set up your ad, you just have to put what your ideal reader's interest is and it will place itself in front of your ideal reader. Currently, Facebook has multiple places where you can put your ads on their platform. Because Facebook owns Instagram, whenever you create an ad on Facebook, you can also create an ad on Instagram.

Campaign Objective on Facebook

When you go to create an ad on Facebook, you start by creating a campaign, which is an overarching term for a set of ads (though a campaign could also be just one ad). For example, you can name your campaign, "Holiday Book Sale," which will be an umbrella for all the ads you run related to any holiday sales you're doing on your books. Or it could just be one ad.

Facebook breaks down ad campaign objectives into three basic categories: awareness, consideration, and conversion. Each campaign has different goals, depending on what you want to get out of your ad:

- Awareness
    - Brand Awareness
    - Reach
- Consideration
    - Traffic
    - Engagement
    - App Installs
    - Video Views
    - Lead Generations
    - Messages
- Conversion
    - Link Conversions

- Catalog Visits
- Store Visits

Most authors use Amazon to sell their books, so I like to recommend selecting "Conversion" as your campaign objective and "Traffic" as your goal. This will allow you to send people to any URL, whether it's your own website or a third party, like Amazon.

Since there are so many different ways you can use and create Facebook ads, you aren't limited to creating a traffic-driven ad, but it would be a good place to start while you're still learning the ropes.

Different Types of Facebook Ad Placement

When you go to set up an ad through Facebook you'll discover very quickly that there are many places your ad can end up and the list is constantly growing.

As I write this, here is the list of some of the options for where your ad can be placed:

- Facebook
    - Feed
    - Instant Articles
    - Right-hand Column
    - Marketplace
    - Stories
- Instagram
    - Feed
    - Stories
- Audience Network (allows you to place ads outside Facebook)
    - Banners
    - Videos

- Messenger
    - Inbox

There are two ways you can go about the placement of your ads. By default, Facebook places your ads for you, meaning it will place the ads everywhere and will put your money into whatever performs best, or you can manually choose where your ads will be placed.

I like to recommend that you manually choose where your ads will be placed because often the size and shape of the graphic for the ad will change. For example, you can't have the same size graphic for a Facebook feed ad as an Instagram story ad. An ad with incorrect sizing won't perform as well because it's not tailored to that space. It's more tedious to make separate graphics for each area you'd like your ad placed, but it will pay off in the end.

When choosing your ad placement, think with your graphic in mind. Where will it look best and will it cause someone to stop and want to click on the ad?

Graphics for Facebook Ads

Remember how we talked about creating graphics in chapter two? It's time to put those skills to work. But before you dive in and start designing your graphic, there's one thing you need to know about Facebook ads: your graphic can't be more than 20% text.

There's no magic way of knowing whether or not your text takes up 20% of the graphic, so the only way to know for sure or not is by submitting the graphic and seeing if Facebook approves the ad. An easy rule to go by is to avoid text in your graphic altogether. The only "text" that should be present is the text that is on the cover of the book. If you do that, you shouldn't run into any issues.

My favorite ads are ones with a 3D mock-up of the paperback with a colored background that fits the genre of the story. If your book has a stunning cover, then it should be able to sell itself. If your book doesn't have a stunning cover...well, why are you investing in ads for your book if you weren't willing to invest in the cover?

The graphic, working in tandem with the book cover, should tell people almost immediately what genre the book is and whether or not it could be something they're interested in.

You can, of course, add text into your graphic, but you will have to do so sparingly, or the ad will be rejected.

Copy for Facebook Ads

Writing the sales copy for your ad will either be the easiest thing or the hardest thing. If you've already invested a lot of time intro perfecting the pitch for your book, then this will be easy. If you still haven't figured out your book's elevator pitch, well... this part may take a little extra work.

There will be two different places Facebook allows you to write something: the "text" and "headline" section.

The text is the most important part and this is where you want to put your one or two sentence pitch of your book that will hopefully entice someone to click the link and read more. This will be similar to what you could write for an Amazon ad, which we'll cover in the next few chapters. Here's an example of sales copy I've used to sell *I am Mercy*:

During the black plague, a young woman struggles to find safety for a family that never loved her. Instead she uncovers a dark magic that changes her life forever.

The headline, on the other hand, is the bolded text that shows up beneath the graphic. If you're familiar with Facebook articles, the bolded title is the "headline." When you're creating your ad, Facebook will create a mock-up of the ad for you as you go, so you can see what your ad will look like on different formats. One of the best headlines you can use is the title of your book and possibliy the genre. For example: *I am Mercy:* YA Historical Fantasy

Sometimes you can add a third type of text to your ad and that's what Facebook considers the "description." The description is the smaller text that appears directly below the headline. You can use this as a place to promote prices, yourself as an author, or the genre of the book if you didn't already promote it in the headline. Here are a few examples of what I could do as a description for *She's Not Here*:

- For sale on Kindle, only $0.99! Limited time only!
- By Amazon Best-Selling Author, Mandi Lynn
- Young Adult Historical Fantasy

When it comes to the headline and description, short and sweet is best. The real selling point of your ad is the regular text section. Everything else should be short enough to grasp someone's attention and make them want to stop and read the ad.

Target Your Facebook Ad to Your Ideal Reader

Whenever someone gets to the stage of marketing where they need to start targeting their ads, they often get a little overwhelmed. Who should you target? How large of a target should you have? Should it be specific or broad?

Stop, breath, and take out your ideal reader profile that you created at the beginning of this book. You can target your ad by using your ideal reader's age, location, gender, languages, and interests. Use that to the full extent. Targeting by interests is where you can get really specific with targeting, because you can target people who follow Facebook pages that are similar to your author page or what you write.

When it comes to interests, I mean only book-related interests. One of my favorite tricks is to use similar authors and books as an interest. You can also tag different terms that have to do with your genre, for example:

- Young adult books

- YA books
- YA fantasy

If you write non-fiction, you can put use the topic of your book as interest tags. For example, "hiking" for a hiking book. Try to get specific with your tags. If your book is specifically on hiking the Appalachian Trail, use "Hiking the Appalachian Trail" or "Hike the AT" as tags. The more specific you can get, the better the targeting for your book will be.

Finding the best targeting method to reach your ideal reader is all about trial and error. Don't invest all your ad money into one place. Play around with ad targeting and see what works best. As you see clicks and sales on your ads, start to invest more into the ad to get more traction on the ad.

You'll notice as you're adjusting your target audience that Facebook will tell you the size of that particular audience. The goal is to be specific, but not so specific that you don't reach a lot of people. My personal rule of thumb is usually 500,000 – 1,000,000 people as an audience size, but I like staying closer to 500,000 people. Anything more than that is too broad and you aren't speaking to your ideal reader. Anything less than that and you aren't targeting enough people and your ad won't get many impressions or clicks.

Your Facebook Ad's Goal

The second part of setting up your ad is choosing what your ad goal is. You've already chosen your campaign's goal, so now it's time to choose the goal for the individual ad.

Here are your goal options:

- Landing page views - Someone clicks on the ad and lets the web page load.

- Link Clicks - Someone clicks on the link, regardless of whether or not they stay long enough to let the page load.
- Impressions - The ad reaches the most people, even if it reaches the same person multiple times
- Daily Unique Reach - It reaches the most unique people.

Each option has a different goal. The first two are great for getting people to click on the ad and visit your book's Amazon page, while the second two are better for exposure of a brand or product, not necessarily sales. If you're making an ad to sell your book, I'd recommend using "Link Clicks" as your goal, since you're leading someone to the sales page of your book. I don't recommend "Landing Page Views" because that's usually reserved for more "interactive experiences" like quizzes, source sign-ups, etc... If you'd like, play around with both and see which one gives you the best results.

Learn What Works Best With A/B Testing on Facebook

Facebook has made it easy to do A/B testing, meaning you can create two ads that are identical, except for one detail, whether that be the sales copy or graphic. This is great for when you'll have two ideas for creating an ad, but aren't sure which would be better.

You'll create your Facebook ad normally, but instead of having one graphic, you have two. Facebook starts off by pushing them both out, but once Facebook sees one performing better than the other, it will automatically stop promoting the low-performing ad and promote the high-performing ad instead so your money is used on the ad that is more successful.

Facebook also auto-targets ad placement. Because Facebook has so many different options for ad placement, they'll start by promoting your ad through all placements you have selected. If they see one placement performing better than another one, they'll stop promoting the low performing one so they can invest the rest of your money into the ad that is performing best.

This saves you money, time, and frustration because Facebook automatically adjusts how the ad shows up.

How Much to Invest in a Facebook Ad

Facebook ads allow you to set either a daily or lifetime budget for your ad. It's hard to say just how much to throw into your ad budget. The more you spend, the more you get out of it. An easy rule of thumb is to start out small, test the waters, and if it goes well, invest more. Start off with a week-long budget of $10-$30 a week and see how that goes. Most times, you never hit your maximum budget since you only pay when someone clicks on your ad. On the bright side, if your ad is getting a lot of clicks, that means you've done a great job placing the ad and designing it in a way that makes people want to click!

If you find you're making a lot of sales, boost your budget to whatever you feel comfortable with. Remember to concentrate on the return on investment. Don't boost your budget if your book sales aren't making back the money you've spent on your ads.

Facebook is PPC, meaning you Pay Per Click. Just because you say your budget is $30 doesn't mean you're going to be paying $30; it just means

$30 is the maximum you're willing to pay. Expect to pay less than what you budget for. If your ad is running and getting very few clicks or impressions, look at your ad again because it means something needs to be fixed. If the targeting seems correct, then consider adjusting the sales copy or graphic.

Why is Your Facebook Ad Failing?

It's easy to get discouraged with paid ads, especially through Facebook, as it can be hard to know at a glance if the ad clicks are converting to sales. You can tell how many people click on the ad, however you won't know for sure if they actually bought the book. If you go to your book sales pages and see no boost in sales, that's an obvious sign that the ads aren't working. Maybe your ads are getting a lot of clicks, but somehow it's falling short when they get to the sales page. This is when you need to consider if something about the sales page is turning them off. Consider all the things we've talked about in book one of this series, *How Your Book Sells Itself*. Is the cover eye-catching? Does the blurb make you want to read more? Or are you lacking book reviews? To get the most out of your money, prepare your graphic, sales copy, and the book itself as much as you can before starting ads.

If your ad isn't getting many clicks, three things could be going wrong:

- The ad placement
- The sales copy
- The graphic

If one of these things isn't correct, it can affect how your ad performs, so try changing things until you've gotten the results you desire. When it comes to making the perfect ad, sometimes the only way to find success is through trial and error. Once again, you only pay for the ad when someone clicks on it. So the good news is, if the ad isn't reaching anyone, you're not losing money. If you're really struggling with your Facebook ads, look at the ads that display on your timeline. Which ones make you want to click on them? What are they doing that you can do as well?

When to Stop Investing in a Facebook Ad

In the intro of this book I mentioned to only run one type of ad at a time, unless you're doing A/B testing. This is so you can see when to stop investing. If you've done everything you can to ensure your ad is the best it can be—you've played around with the placement, graphics, sales copy, and the sales page—and it's still not converting to sales, it may be time to pull the plug. Sometimes paid ads just aren't worth the investment. This is especially true with a book that is in a competitive market.

Even if an ad is converting to sales, you still need to pay attention to ROI (return on investment). If you spent $60 on a Facebook ad, but only made $50 in sales when the ad was running, it's time to remember why you decided to run this ad. Is your goal to expose your book to more people or to make more money in book sales? If you want to run ads solely for the purpose of exposure, than a $10 loss may not be bad, but if you're running the ads to make money off your book than you're doing just the opposite.

BETHANY'S TIPS:

I've only ever run a few Facebook ads (and Instagram ads) personally. Why? Because I found that my audience is hardly ever on the Facebook platform, so advertising there was a waste of money for me. When it comes to genres like non-fiction, adult fiction, and maybe even romance, Facebook can be a fantastic place for ads, but for someone like me who mainly writes YA, the majority of my audience just isn't active on Facebook.

I mention this because I think it's extremely important to choose advertising strategies that benefit your book and your target audience/ideal reader. When you set up your ideal reader in chapter one, where did you decide that they spent their time online? Knowing this can help you decide where to invest your time, energy, and especially finances.

In my case, my readers are on Instagram more than anywhere else online (except maybe YouTube). So, I also tested out Instagram ads briefly. While I enjoyed the process, I soon discovered that, at least back when I was experimenting with running Instagram ads, the ads were only visible as long as they were running.

I racked up tons of likes and comments, only to find that once the ad ended, all of that hard work and interest generated on the post disappeared! It was a frustrating surprise to say the least! Personally, that turned me off of doing Instagram ads, but in the future, I may reconsider. Especially during specific events, such as a book release week or a cover reveal or a special offer of some kind, I think an Instagram ad could still be valuable for me, and also to you—if your audience is there.

When it comes to Facebook and Instagram ads, it's my opinion that they're especially helpful during big events, like those I mentioned above. While Amazon ads can run non-stop and be continuously helpful, bursts of ads on Facebook and Instagram during important events can help you not spend money too frequently, while still having the rewards of increased awareness and interest in your book.

CHAPTER 7:
UNDERSTANDING AMAZON ADVERTISING

"Stopping advertising to save money is like stopping your watch to save time."

– Henry Ford

AMAZON ADS ARE my personal favorite type of ad. They are the most direct way to access your ideal reader. Someone will only see an Amazon Ad if they're already shopping on Amazon. That's right, these people are *ready to buy*. They come with credit card in hand, ready to make a purchase. They aren't scrolling through social media or checking their emails, they're already actively searching for something to buy, so now your book just needs to sound interesting enough to add it to their cart.

I've saved the best for last and I'm going to be using four chapters to walk you through marketing on Amazon.

While placing ads on Amazon can be one of the most beneficial ways to promote your books, it can also be the most confusing and complicated. It's easy to set up Amazon ads incorrectly. But once you understand how the platform works, you'll find your book sales increasing.

A lot of authors are hesitant to use Amazon ads because they're afraid to invest money into something they don't fully understand. Take it from me. The very first Amazon ad I set up was for my second novel, *I am Mercy*. I set up my ad to have a daily budget of $1. Because I didn't know what I was doing, I did a lot of guesswork and played it safe. But because I played it safe, my ad didn't reach as many people as I had wanted it to. I only got one sale at the end of it, meaning I sold a $3.99 book. And how much did I spend on my ad? $0.19.

That's it! Less than twenty cents and I sold one book!

Now, mind you, I still didn't know what I was doing, so I turned off the ad and called it a day. To me, Amazon was a gamble. I had placed a bet and I won, no matter how small the prize was.

I don't want you to feel like this. I want you to not only understand how Amazon Advertising works, but to conquer it.

What Makes Amazon Ads Work?

Targeting is the secret behind your success when it comes to ads on Amazon. Never has your ideal reader profile been so important. We're going to take all that information you collected and use it to target your ideal readers as they're searching for things to buy on Amazon.

The way Amazon uses targeting is through keywords. This is different from the keywords that you use when you're first setting up your book on Kindle Direct Publishing. The keywords you use on Amazon ads are words that your potential reader might type into their Amazon search if they're looking for a book like yours. While you may use the same keywords that are listed on your book's Kindle Direct Publishing page, you'll want many more keywords than that for a successful ad.

I've heard some authors say that there's no point in doing an Amazon ad unless you have at least 1,000 keywords. While I'm sure having that many keywords will help, a well-targeted Amazon ad campaign will be closer to 200 keywords or more. That may sound like a lot, but you'll discover in the next chapter just how quickly your list of keywords can grow and you'll easily be able to come up with a list of 200 keywords. The reason why you need so many keywords is because otherwise your targeting will be too niche and you'll notice your ad won't gain much traction. There are rare instances where you can make an ad work with only 30 keywords, but that's not common.

Where Do Ads Show Up?

There are two different types of ads you can choose from when you're on Amazon: Sponsored

Product Ads and Lock Screen ads. Both serve very different purposes, so you'll want to choose the type of ad that best fits your goal is for that ad.

Sponsored Product Ads

This is the most popular and usually most successful form of ad. This is the ad that shows up in search results and is targeted based on what keywords you choose. For example, let's say a reader is on Amazon and they search "young adult fantasy." Along with the regular search results, you'll also notice a few sponsored results, which are the sponsored product ads. If you choose "young adult fantasy" as one of your keywords, then your book may pop up as a sponsored ad. We'll talk more about Sponsored Product Ads in chapter nine because it's one of the most complex to set up, but it can also be one of the most rewarding.

Kindle Lock Screen Ad

Amazon used to offer Product Display ads, but that option is no longer available and has been replaced by Lock Screen Ads. If you were familiar with Product Displays, Lock Screen Ads work in a similar way. Instead of pasting in a long list of keywords, you select the genre you'd like to advertise your book with. If someone is reading a book of that genre on their Kindle e-reader or Fire tablet, the ad will pop up in one of two places:

1. Full screen ad on the lock screen
2. Banner ad on the Kindle homepage

If someone wants to read your book they just have to click on the ad to be brought to the book's purchase page.

Kindle Lock Screen Ads are brand-new, so it's possible that Amazon will change and shift the requirements as time goes on. For myself, I found one big downfall to the Lock Screen Ads: genre targeting isn't a small enough niche. When I went in to set up an ad for *She's Not Here*, I selected the thriller genre, but I wasn't impressed with the selection of niche genres underneath thriller:

1. Conspiracies
2. Heist
3. Horror
4. Kidnapping
5. Legal
6. Murder
7. Organized crime
8. Paranormal
9. Vigilante justice

What about psychological thrillers? That's an important niche genre, but it's missing from the targeting options. There were so many niches I wanted to target (such as dark contemporary or medical thriller) that were also missing from their list.

I also hesitate with Lock Screen Ads because if I'm reading on my kindle, I'm not looking to buy more books. How many times have you been on YouTube and skipped an ad without watching it? That's how I see the Lock Screen Ads. Now, at the same time, people shop for new books on their Kindle all the time, so it could lead to many sales, so try it out if you'd like, especially if you find your book's main genre is listed as a targeting option!

How Much Do Amazon Ads Cost?

The best part of Amazon ads is that you only pay when someone clicks on them. You could set your budget for $100, but if you only get a few clicks, you'll never get anywhere close to paying $100.

This means if you make a terrible ad and there are no clicks on it, you didn't have to pay a cent! This is called Pay Per Click (PPC). This also means that if you have a daily budget of $5-$10 that you probably won't be spending that much on a daily basis. You *might* spend that much if you did an amazing job with your targeting and set the perfect bid amount, but that's rare.

Which brings us to bids…

What Is a Bid?

A bid is the amount of money you're willing to "bid" to make your ad show up instead of someone else's. But it goes a little further than that because Amazon values two things:

1. The amount of money they make
2. The amount of engagement an ad receives

A post with high engagement is valuable to Amazon because that means customers are getting what they're looking for.

Amazon wants ads that are relevant to their customers.

Amazon wants to build a good customer experience and for people to discover items that are perfect them, which is why Amazon rewards ads that do just that. Plus, the more clicks an ad gets, the more money they make off that ad. With that said, if you're targeting an audience that isn't relevant to your book, even if you put in a high bid, you won't get clicks and Amazon won't run your ad. To help explain, here's an example:

Advertiser A bids $0.75 and has 4 clicks

Advertiser B bids $0.50 and has 10 clicks

Advertiser C bids $0.25 and has 15 clicks

What does Amazon make from each advertiser?

Advertiser A: $3

Advertiser B: $5

Advertiser C: $3.75

Now between the three advertisers, who's Amazon going to choose? Advertiser B, because when you multiply their bid times their number of clicks, Amazon makes the most profit. This goes to show that the highest bid isn't the only factor that determines whether your ad succeeds.

You should always experiment with your bids and sales copy. Modify them to see how you can get the most out of your ads. Which brings me to my next point:

Amazon Ads Shouldn't Be "Set It and Forget It"

When you have an ad campaign on Amazon, you have to keep an eye on it to know what's working and what isn't. You'll need to review it every day or so, to know when you should increase or decrease your bids so you aren't spending too much, but also to see if your ad is still showing up for keywords.

Predicting Your Ad's ROI

Let's talk about what everyone is thinking. Is it worth it? Can I really sell a lot of books using Amazon ads? The simple answer is yes. If you take the time to learn how to set up your ads and target them correctly, you will likely see success. You'll not only break even in your spending, but you'll make money off your books and find new readers who would otherwise never discover your books.

When it comes to predicting your ROI, it's not a straightforward answer. Just like how you'll have to adjust your bid amount, the money you make off your books will vary.

Getting The Most Money Out Of Your Ads

There are a few things to keep in mind that will help you make more money off your Amazon ads. This goes further than just creating an ad on Amazon. The four best practices listed below touch upon how you can create more income for yourself as an indie author, make the most of your Amazon Ads, and how one book sale can result in more sales down the line.

1. Having Multiple Formats

By default, your ads on Amazon will always take customers to the Kindle edition of your book, but that doesn't stop them from buying the book in paperback, hardcover, or even in audiobook if they'd like. Some readers are particular about what format they prefer to read, which is why it's best to have multiple options available, even if you make the most money off your ebook edition.

2. Writing a Series

If you have a book that's part of a large series, it's best to run ads for the first book. Each time you have a new release in the series you can run another ad for the first book to draw in new readers! This will get the reader hooked into the series and they'll continue reading on even after they've finished the first book. A great thing to help sell an entire series is to add a link to buy the next book in the series at the end of a previous book in the series. If a reader loves book one in a series and you include the link to buy book two at the end, you'll increase your odds of them buying book two.

3. Writing Books in the Same Genre

When you write books that are all in the same genre, it works in a similar way as when someone gets hooked on a series. If you have multiple books in one genre, refer to those books at the beginning and end of your book so a reader who enjoys one book will seek out the other similar books you've written.

4. Including an Opt-in or Upsell

You usually only see this type of example in non-fiction books, but you can also find it in fiction books as a way to gather email addresses for your author newsletter. The book could make a mention to a helpful template or a deleted scene from a story for a fiction story. In order to get the template, you have to visit the author's website and sign up for their email list. Templates are just one example of an opt-in and if you read book two in this series, *Grow Your Author Platform*, you know the many different types of email opt-ins there are.

For non-fiction books, an author could be talking all about how to start a business and then at the end of the book they would mention their online course or webinar. This is called an upsell, when you offer something for a small price so your audience gets a taste of what you have to offer, then there will be an offer to upgrade to the "full product" at a higher price.

These are just some examples of why authors will run Amazon ads for heavily discounted or free books. They aren't looking to make money off the book itself, but instead off the offer within the book, like an online course, gaining subscribers for an email list, or introducing readers to one book so they'll read other books they've written.

Feel like you're starting to understand how Amazon ads work? Great! Because we're about to kick things into high gear!

BETHANY'S TIPS:

I have periodically run "Sponsored Product Ads" during book releases and even just to *experiment a few times. I've also tried the old "Product Display Ad" that Amazon used to have before the Kindle Lock Screen Ad. Just FYI—this Product Display ad had a $100 minimum and so does the "Lock Screen Ad."*

After quite a bit of research, I discovered that authors rarely spent that much, and if they did, it was only because the income was even higher. In that case, it was a higher threshold, but with a higher payout.

I wouldn't be surprised if the same was true of the new Lock Screen Ad version. However, I just don't see a Lock Screen as being quite as effective to be honest. When I picture reading a book on a Kindle, I know that personally I have zero interest in any pop-ups or anything besides the book that I'm reading.

So, is it worth it?

My best advice would be to scour the internet for people who have braved this type of ad. There are always people willing to speak about their experience. Amazon could change their ads again tomorrow and try a new style, and this advice would still hold true—find someone who's forged the way and ask them if they think it's worth it. Or, if you're feeling brave, take a chance and try it yourself!

CHAPTER 8:
COLLECTING DATA

"Without big data, you are blind and deaf and in the middle of a freeway."

– Geoffrey Moore

IT'S TIME TO start collecting your keywords to create your Amazon Ad. All this could happen before you log into your Amazon Advertising account, because you need to collect data before you start creating an ad. There's no point in going into the account until you have all the information required. If you collect the needed information before you log in, setting up the ad will feel like a breeze and be much less intimidating.

There are three things you need to do before creating a campaign on Amazon:

1. Create a list of keywords
2. Write your sales copy
3. Review your book's listing on Amazon

When I say "review your book's listing" I mean you want to make sure the sales page on Amazon is as good as it can be. This means the book needs to have reviews and that the description of the book is enticing to someone who's never heard of you or your book before. I'll go into more detail about refining your book's sales page later.

How to Choose Successful Keywords

Creating your list of Amazon keywords is time-consuming but it will be worth it, plus you'll understand your book's niche and genre better by the end of sifting through all the keywords. A good ad will have at the least 200 keywords. Amazon allows a maximum of 1,000. That may seem like a lot, but you might be surprised to find you have to narrow down your list. When I created a keyword list for *Essence*, I had over 1,300 keywords to work through before I picked the best keywords for my book.

Now this, like everything else in Amazon ads, is a working list. As you adjust things later on, you'll add and remove keywords as you see fit.

Here's my process for collecting keywords:

1. **Open an excel sheet** and write down all the genre-based keywords you can think of.

What types of words would your ideal reader type into Amazon to a find a book like yours? I'm not talking about your book's title or your author name, I'm talking genre-specific words. Get as niche as possible and list all different variations of the keywords/genre that you can think of. Put each keyword on a new line in your excel sheet.

2. **Open an incognito page on your web browser on Amazon** and set the department to "Kindle Store." An incognito page removes any data that your computer has collected from you about your search history, so an incognito page will always give the best results of what *other* people search for. Start typing in the keywords

you've come up with so far. See the suggestions Amazon gives you? If they apply to your book (and you don't have them already), write them down. If Amazon isn't giving you suggestions, put a letter. "Contemporary A" for example could give you results like "contemporary adult" and "contemporary adult romance." Do this for every keyword and work through the whole alphabet if you have to.

What you're trying to come up with is a list of long-tail keywords (AKA longer keyword phrases composed of more than one word). The more specific your keywords are, the more successful you will be at targeting your ideal reader. The more long-tail your keywords are, the less competition you'll have from other advertisers, which means the less you'll have to pay.

3. **Visit the best-seller list of your book's genre** and start writing down the titles of the books in the top twenty slots. Also write down each author's name as a separate keyword. Using book titles and author names means that if someone types in that book or author, your book could show up as an ad on that search results page. If you're not familiar with Amazon ads this may feel weird or even like you're cheating the system. But it's not only normal to do this, it's encouraged! This is how you'll generate most of your keywords. Visit all the best-selling pages for every genre your book fits

into and write down all the potential keywords.

4. **Visit the recent releases best-seller page** and do the same thing. The books on this list are great because they're fresh, people are actively searching for them, and other advertisers probably haven't jumped on using them as keywords yet.

5. **Visit the "Customers Also Bought" section** of your book's sales page. Write down the books your customers also bought because this is basically a built-in comp title recommendation. Your readers like your book, and they also liked this book.

6. **View your "Similar Authors" section** of your Amazon Author page and write down the authors. If they write in the same genre as you, write down their books as well.

7. **Repeat these steps with comp titles.** Using the comp titles you established in chapter two of this book, repeat steps three through six.

When you're exploring deep into Amazon like this it can be easy to start writing down every book and author under the sun, especially when you aren't sure what some books are about, but try to stay genre focused. When in doubt about a keyword, think about what your book is really about. What is the theme? What's the main selling point of your book? Like I mentioned before, coming up with a list of keywords can help you understand your book's genre better. Sometimes as you follow these steps you may realize the books on this list aren't as similar to your book as you thought.

If you realize your book isn't actually in the right genre, then by all means, go into your KDP account and update the genre(s). That's the glory of self-publishing. You can change things at any time. Did you discover your contemporary novel was actually a coming-of-age novel? Change it. My favorite part of this exercise is learning from how books are placed in their genres.

After I set up my first ad for *Essence*, I changed all the genres it was listed under, as well as giving it a few more specific keywords in the KDP description, which helped my book show up better in search and be placed in the correct area on Amazon.

You'll always be learning, so don't be afraid to change things or even experiment a little, just to see how it benefits your book.

As a review, your ad keywords should be pulled from the following categories:

- Genre-based keywords
- "Customers also bought" books & authors
- Top 20 books and authors in your genre(s)
- "Similar Authors" listed in your bio
- Comp titles & authors

There is a shortcut to collecting all your keywords, but I've waited this long to tell you about the shortcut because the shortcut is useless if you don't understand how keywords work in the first place. I think the above steps are some of the best things you can do as an author to understand your book's place on Amazon and how it should be categorized. Understanding how Amazon works helps you work with Amazon, rather than against it. Once you figure that out, then you can take shortcuts.

And that shortcut is the Publisher Rocket software (formerly known as KDP rocket). This software was created by Dave Chesson of Kindlepreneur. The software allows you to do a few things:

1. Look up keywords to list on your book's sales page
2. Look up categories to list your book under
3. See how other books in your genre are doing in comparison
4. Generate keywords for Amazon Ads

That last part is the most exciting. Essentially it takes all the steps we talked above, and does the work for you.

How To Use Publisher Rocket

It's not a simple plug in and go, but it's a lot easier than creating the list yourself. When I wanted to create an ad for *Essence*, I used Rocket to generate all my keywords and the entire process took about a half-hour, whereas if I'd done it manually, it could've taken hours.

Here are the steps I took:

1. **Book genre**—*Essence* breaks down into three major genres: coming of age, young adult fantasy, young adult paranormal. I searched each of those genres in Rocket, exported the lists, and saved them on my computer.

2. **Find comp titles**—I took all my major comp titles/comp title authors and entered them

into the Rocket software. Again, exporting each individual list of keywords and saving them.

3. **Review for missing keywords**—Sometimes those first two steps will generate more than enough keywords for you, but if you feel like something is missing, continue plugging major keywords into the Rocket software.

4. **Combine keywords**—Right now all your keywords will be in separate excel documents. Copy and paste all the keywords into one excel sheet. Delete duplicates. Excel can do this for you, so you don't have to do it manually. Go to the "Data" tab and select "Delete Duplicates." From there sort

cells A through Z to remove any blank cells. You'll also find this command under the "Data" tab.

5. **Delete keywords**—Go through your list of keywords and delete any that seem out of place. When I created my list for *Essence,* I noticed Game of Thrones was on it. While both books are fantasy, I deleted the keyword because that was the only thing that was similar about the two books.

By the end of all this you should have a list that is at least a few hundred words long, but hopefully less than one thousand words.

Writing Copy For Your Amazon Ads

The second step to preparing your book for advertising on Amazon is writing your copy.

Writing your ads for Amazon will probably be the hardest copy to write, because you don't have any graphic that goes with your ad. When an Amazon ad pops up, it's just the book cover and a line that will hook someone into buying your book. You have only 150 characters to do this. This brings the one-sentence pitch to a whole new level.

When you're writing your ad, think about your novel's hook. When you wrote the first chapter of your novel, you tried to hook your reader right away so they read on to chapter two. Ad copy is the same way. You need to hook people with what's at stake. What's the selling point of the novel?

Don't misrepresent your book, because you pay for the ad if someone clicks on it, but you don't make any money unless they actually buy the book. If you misrepresent your book, they'll click on the ad, but then get to your book's page on Amazon and see it's not for them, wasting their time and your money.

Think of your elevator pitch that you use to tell people about your novel. An elevator pitch is usually only a few sentences long, so try taking those few sentences and slimming them down even more. And make those one to three sentences a cliffhanger. Give the reader a reason to stop and add your book to their cart so they can find out what happens.

Take Campaign Targeting Even Further

If you feel like you can pitch your book multiple ways depending on which niche audience you're referring to, you can make your campaigns even more targeted. Take the long list of keywords you made in this chapter and follow these steps:

1. **Topics** - What type of topics do all the keywords break down into? If your book is fiction, it would break down into the book's three major genres. If your book is non-fiction, you can break it down by major topics. For example, a book on writing could have these types of topics: writing technique, writing the first draft, editing, and so on. Looking at your keywords, you should see a theme and similar topics that you can group keywords into. Go through all the keywords in your list and sort them into the topics you come up with. Which leads us to step two…

2. **Write Copy** - Now your keywords are even more niche. You can target very specific people to see this ad. Write up sales copy for each category and you can run a campaign for each category, making your targeting even more spot-on.

A/B Testing Your Amazon Ad

If you have two ways you want to pitch your novel, you can always try A/B testing it. When you begin your campaign on Amazon, you'll use the first version of copy and start your campaign, then duplicate the campaign and change only the sales copy. Let both ads run and whichever performs better is the one you should use going forward.

This is something I'm currently doing for an ad I'm running for the second book in *Marketing for Authors: Grow Your Author Platform*. Both ads were set up exactly the same, but the sales copy was different:

A) Learn how to sell your books using your website, email list, blog and more!

B) "If you're struggling to market not only your books, but yourself as an author, this book was written with you in mind." ~Amazon Reviewer

So far, both ads have been getting clicks, but ad A has gotten 62 clicks while ad B only got 16. I ended up pausing the campaign for ad B, and I'm going to be creating a third ad, ad C, using the copy from ad A, but changing the targeting for the ad to see if that makes any difference. My goal is to constantly make small changes by comparing two ads and always seeing if I can get one to perform better than the other, as well as to know *why* it performed better.

Review Your Book's Listing on Amazon

This is the final thing you need to do before creating your ad campaign, because if your book's sales page isn't correct then someone may click on your ad, get to the sales page, and not buy the book. So what can stop someone from buying your book once they click on the ad? There are five things that can come into play:

- Book description errors
- Book cover
- Reviews
- Book Genre
- Book Keywords

The Book Description

Also called the back-cover blurb, this is your selling point for the book. Someone liked the one-sentence pitch you wrote to get them to click on the ad, but if your synopsis doesn't wow them in the same way, they're not going to buy the book.

Because you're self-published you have the power to change your book's description whenever you want. When I made an ad for *Essence,* the ad was getting a ton of clicks but no sales. I realized the problem was the book's description. I have the habit of describing *Essence* in a vague way because I don't want to give anything away, but when I tell my readers more of what's at stake and reveal just a little bit more, it makes the book sound much more interesting.

The Book Cover

Oh yes, people judge a book by its cover. If it's not pretty, people will assume the inside of your book isn't all that pretty either. The cover should also match the genre of your book or you'll create confusion as to what the book is really about.

I currently work with indie authors to design book covers, so if you're interested in giving your book a face lift, visit: www.stoneridgebooks.com

Book Reviews

This is where things get tricky. If someone stumbles across a book on Amazon that they've never heard of and it doesn't have any reviews, or it only has a small handful of reviews, then that person may not buy the book. Reviews encourage people to buy.

It's a sad cycle. You need book sales to get reviews, but people won't buy your book if it doesn't have reviews. The easiest way to break the cycle is to reach out to bloggers and other reviewers and give them a free ebook in exchange for an honest review. Let them know that you'd like the book to be reviewed on Amazon specifically (sometimes bloggers will only post the review on their blog).

If you have a small handful of reviews, you can highlight some of your favorites by adding them to your book's description. At the end of your description on Amazon, put "What Amazon readers had to say:" and then list one-sentence quotes from positive reviews. You can even quote reviews from blogs, Goodreads, or anywhere else that reviews pop up; just make sure to state where the review is from.

Book Genre & Keywords

I first published *Essence* when I was seventeen, so I didn't know much about placing my book properly on Amazon. Like I mentioned earlier, after creating my first ad I realized my book could be placed in a better, more niche genre on Amazon, as well as have better KDP keywords. While buyers don't really see a book's genre and keywords, they do affect how your book is placed on the ranking scale and how Amazon targets your ad for you.

If the keywords you created for your ad don't match the keywords you listed for the book on KDP you're working against yourself; the book won't show up in search properly and the ad won't get as much engagement, thus Amazon won't push the ad as much.

Doing all this research for Amazon ads is a lot of work but you'll understand your book better and what you really want to market. After you set up an ad once, you'll find it easier to do more ads in the future.

BETHANY'S TIPS:

Like Mandi said, the book itself has a lot of power to make or break sales. We talk about this so much in How Your Book Sells Itself, and we can honestly guarantee your ads will perform better if you set your book up for success with these 10 elements:

1. *The genre*
2. *The cover*
3. *The title*
4. *The blurb (back cover synopsis)*
5. *The tagline*
6. *The formatting*
7. *The editing*

8. The keywords

9. The categories

10. Your marketing mindset

I won't waste your time regurgitating all this information from the first book in the series, since you can easily go check it out if you'd like to know more. But one thing I will add to this list, that will also affect sales and hugely impact if your ads are successful or not, is something we've already touched on briefly in chapter five, when we discussed Goodreads Giveaways: reviews.

I know you don't have a lot of control over this aspect. In fact, you might think you don't have any. But the truth is, the people who genuinely enjoy your book will also genuinely want to support you and tell others how much they loved it. Sometimes the only thing stopping them from telling the world is simply a lack of awareness that this is helpful.

Sometimes all you need to do to change this awareness, is ask.

So, don't be afraid to include a simple request for reviews in your marketing strategies. Especially around a book release. Ask your newsletter subscribers to review the book on Amazon. Use social media to thank everyone who leaves reviews and maybe even give them personal shout outs.

Add another note to your calendar to post a gentle reminder two weeks after release, and again after your book has been out for a month. Keep sharing the (good) reviews, or the number of reviews, or any other fresh, new, and authentic posts about reviews that you can come up with.

As long as you don't spam your readers, I feel confident that the people who enjoyed your story will come out of the woodwork to support you and be more than happy to do so!

CHAPTER 9:
CREATING AN AMAZON AD

"Nobody reads ads. People read what interests them, and sometimes it's an ad."

—Howard Luck Gossage

THERE ARE TWO places you can create Amazon ads. Through KDP or through Amazon Advertising.

Amazon recently went through a rebranding. What used to be known as Amazon Marketing Services (AMS) is now called Amazon's Advertising Console and their marketing platform as a whole is called "Amazon Advertising." I'm mentioning this just in case after you read this book you move on to read other articles about Amazon ads and encounter the acronym "AMS" instead of Advertising Console.

To access your Advertising Console through KDP, go to your bookshelf, find the book you want to advertise, and select "Promote and Advertise." KDP will walk you through a few steps before bringing you to the console page to create your campaign.

Creating Your First Campaign Through KDP

1. Select the "**Promote and Advertise**" button for the book on the KDP bookshelf.

2. Select "**Create an Ad Campaign**."

3. **Choose a campaign type.** This is where you decide which type of ad you'd like to run: a Sponsored Product Ad or Lock Screen Ad. From there a screen will open where you'll input all your campaign information. In this example, I'll be referring to a Sponsored Product Ad.

4. **Name your campaign** something that will make it easily identifiable. I like my campaign names to have the title of the book being promoted and the date it will start. I usually keep a screenshot

of all the information about my campaigns, so if a campaign performs well or poorly, I can name the campaign by the date to avoid mixing them up.

5. **Select your start and end date.** You can schedule your campaign for a specific day (such as when you have a price promotion running) or you can have it start right away. I don't like choosing end dates for my campaigns because I like to keep a close eye on it and make adjustments over time. I only end a campaign if it isn't working anymore and sometimes it can take weeks before I decide if an ad is doing well or not.

6. **Choose your daily budget.** I like to have a daily of budget of $5-10 because I usually only end up

spending a dollar or so. Remember, you're only paying when someone clicks on the ad.

7. **Select manual targeting.** This is so you can add in all those keywords you worked so hard to collect.

8. **Choose custom ad text** so you can paste in your sales copy.

9. **Choose your product.** If you started from the KDP bookshelf you'll notice your book is already selected. If you start from Amazon Advertising you'll need to choose the book you want to run an ad for.

10. **Choose your campaign bidding strategy.** This is actually something that's brand new as I write

this. The bidding strategies are in beta phase, so some of what I say may change. You'll have three bid strategies to choose from:

- **Dynamic bids - down only:** if your ad *isn't* likely to convert sales it will automatically lower your bid which will replace your ad with another.
- **Dynamic bids - up and down:** as well as lowering your bid, if your ad *is* likely to convert sales your bid will automatically be raised.
- **Fixed bids:** nothing will be adjusted. Whatever you set as your bids will stay your bids.

In the past, bids were all the first option: dynamic bids - down only. I'm currently experimenting with the up and down feature in hopes that this will help me win bids I otherwise would have lost. I suggest you experiment as well and see what works best for you.

11. **Set negative keywords.** If there are keywords or products you don't want your ad showing up for, you can list it in your negative keywords. For example, if you write an action adventure novel but you don't want people searching for action movies to be targeting in an ad, you can list the word "movie" as a negative keyword. At this time, I don't put any negative keywords in my ads, because even if my book pops up in a movie search result, odds are my book matches the genre of the movie, so my audience would be more or less the same. It's the same story, just told in a different format.

12. **Choose your bid type.** There are two ways you can go about choosing your bid type and it depends on what your goals are:

- *High impressions*—If you want a lot of people to see your ad, then using the suggested bid is your best bet to have your ad placed. However, a high bid means that you'll meet your daily budget of clicks much faster, which means you may need to raise your daily budget to avoid missing opportunities.

- *More clicks*—If you'd like as many clicks as possible, you can chose a lower bid amount and if you targeted your ad correctly, Amazon will still place your ad, just not as frequently. Because your bid is lower, you can afford to have more clicks a day, which means more potential sales.

13. **Target your ad** by either pasting in all the keywords you've collected or selecting book genres if you're doing a Lock Screen Ad. If you're pasting in keywords you'll notice there are suggested bids for each keyword. Feel free to adjust your default bid as you'd like. I usually like to set my bids a few cents below the suggested bid and raise it later on if I don't see the ad making any impressions.

14. **Paste in the sales copy** you wrote up earlier and preview your ad.

15. If everything looks good, **hit "Launch Campaign."**

And that's all there is to it! You'll need to wait for your ad to be approved, but for now you're done.

How to Read Your Amazon Ad Stats

Every time you log into Amazon Advertising you'll be brought to the dashboard/console page. You'll be able to see a quick overview of all your campaigns: which are active, when they started, when they will end, what their budget is, and so on.

Let's break it down a little further so you fully understand your ad campaigns:

- **Spend**—The amount you've spent so far on the campaign.
- **Orders**—How many orders have resulted from the campaign. It can take up to 12 hours for orders to show up, but the amount you spend shows up right away. This means it could look like you spent money but didn't make any sales because the information takes longer to update.

- **Sales**—This also takes 12 hours to update, but there's a twist to this one. The sales is the total amount of money generated from a sale. This means if your ebook costs $3.99, that's the number that will show up. But as you know, you only make 30-70% of royalties on each sale, so take that into account when you see this number.

- **ACOS**—This is Advertising Costs of Sales. This is a percentage calculated when you divide the total ad spend by total sales. The lower your percentage, the better.

- **Actions**—You'll notice the option to "Copy." This is how you duplicate your ad if you'd like to do A/B testing or decide you like an older ad.

- **Impressions**—this is how many people have seen your ad.

At the very top of your dashboard you'll notice the option to add metrics. Here are a few more metrics you can view on your dashboard if you'd like:

- **Clicks**—the amount of people that have clicked on your ad
- **Cost-Per-Click** —The average amount of money you spend when someone clicks on an ad
- **Click-Through-Rate (CTR)** —The percentage of people that view the book's sales page after clicking on the ad. The higher the number, the better.

Since it takes time for sales and orders to be reported, don't get discouraged if you don't make anything at first. I suggest letting the campaign run anywhere from three to five days before you try changing anything. In the next chapter, we're going to talk about how to take data from your report and use it to optimize your campaign.

BETHANY'S TIPS:

Personal story time: I got so discouraged when I first set up Amazon ads. Mandi is right. It takes time, testing, and tons of patience to figure out a successful ad on Amazon. At the time of publishing this book, I've only done about a dozen different Amazon ads, so I'm by no means an expert like Mandi, but a few things have caught my attention as I've done ads, that I'd like to share:

1. Sometimes an "automatic targeting" ad can actually be more effective than a "manual targeting" ad. This is because if the ad is set up by Kindle itself, there are certain keywords like "kindle" that Amazon is allowed to use, while you, the author, are not allowed to use if you do manual targeting. So, in some cases, automatic targeting reaches an entirely different set of search terms! Also you can click into an Automatic Campaign to see how it's performing, which allows you to discover tons of potential long-tail keywords you may have never guessed people are searching for! This is another reason that Automatic Campaigns can be great for beginners especially, since they can help you learn good keywords that work for your book.

2. *It can be hard to tell effectiveness of an ad right away though. Which leads to my next point.*

3. It is so hard to tell if an Amazon ad is working, when you only have a few days of data available. It can be so tempting to stop the ad if it doesn't look successful. In some cases, I've done that. In others, I wasn't online as much, forgot about the ad, and came back after a week, or two, or three—only to find that the ad had taken off! Like Mandi mentioned, certain things, like page reads, can be hard to calculate right away. While a click is counted immediately, a sale might not be counted for 48 hours. That means that for two days it could look like you spent money without making anything, only to find out on the following day that the ad was far more effective than it first appeared.

4. I've also noticed that it's normal to have a lot of duds. It takes practice. I'd started to lose faith in ads, thinking maybe they weren't worth my time in the first place, only to stumble across other successful indie authors like Chris Fox, Mark Dawson, or Joanna Penn, who all swear by them. Some indie authors even show you their ad dashboards and prove just how effective they can be! That was enough to give me hope and help me press on, until I started seeing better results in my own ads.

5. Because of all the above, I urge you to take it slow and start out with small bids. Yes, it could be fun to go all in on that Lock Screen Ad for $100. But I think ads are really similar to writing in general. It takes practice before they're any good. It takes a lot of editing. So, in *the beginning, just assume that your ads aren't your best work and that you'll get better, and treat them as practice or "trial runs." AKA don't spend too much.*

CHAPTER 10:
OPTIMIZING AMAZON ADS

"It's much easier to double your business by doubling your conversion rate than doubling your traffic."

– Bryan Eisenberg

LET'S GET TO optimizing! Odds are, your first campaign isn't going to do so hot. It takes practice to understand how Amazon ads work and what you need to do. Once you see your ad getting a little traction, it's time to give it a closer look to see how you can help it perform even better.

Amazon ads need to be monitored on a regular basis, meaning you should be checking on them every few days to see how they're performing. Some authors prefer to check their ads on a daily basis, but at the very least I'd recommend checking on it every three days. I'd suggest letting an ad run for at least two to three weeks before you completely pause an ad. Before you decide to give up on an ad, there are plenty of things you can do to improve it, which is what this chapter is all about!

There are some common areas where things could have gone wrong. On the campaign homepage, click on the name of your campaign to view all the details. Under the "Ad" tab, view all your metrics. Does anything seem lower than it should be? Are you spending too much? Are your impressions low? How many clicks do you have? Here are some quick solutions to some of the most common problems:

If You Spent Too Much Money

It's possible the keywords you selected were too popular, meaning that in order for your ad to show up, you had to have a high bid. Keywords with high-competition are often dominated by traditional publishers who have much larger budgets, so when you're self-published with an ebook for only $3.99, it's not worth it to put in the top bid for a competitive keyword. A quick an esay solution is to try to stay away from pupular keywords.

If You Didn't Get Many Clicks

Your ad got thousands of impressions but only a few clicks? This could be that the sales copy for your ad isn't interesting enough to cause someone to want to buy the book. Try adjusting the sales copy and see what happens from there. If that still doesn't work check your keywords and make sure you're targeting the right audience. Either way, the good news is you haven't lost any money because you only pay when someone clicks.

If the Click-Through Rate is Low

The click-through rate of your ad is the number of people who clicked on the ad divided by the number of times your ad has been shown to people. If your ad made 3,000 impressions but only 10 people clicked on it, that's a click-through rate of about 0.03%. There's no magic number of "this is what your click-through rate should be," but the higher the better. If you want a number to shoot for, a good click-through rate on an ad is sometimes considered 2%. To improve your click-through rate, make your ad sales copy even more interesting. Hook them into your book and tell them why they should click on the ad.

If People Still Aren't Buying the Book

Say everything I've already talked about is fine—your ad has good impressions and a handful of people are clicking on the ad, and even the click-through-rate is pretty good—but people still aren't buying the book. What's going on? This means your book's page on Amazon needs some attention. Is the cover and summary impressive enough to cause someone to buy the book? If your book is missing the wow factor that causes people to buy, it's time to adjust.

If Nothing Happened

You've been bracing yourself for something, for anything to happen, but nothing! No impressions and no clicks. Two things could have gone wrong here. The sales copy you wrote to go with your ad might not have been interesting enough, which means no one clicked on the ad, and therefore Amazon didn't want to display the ad because they didn't feel it was a good match. Or you might not have had a long enough list of keywords. If you only had a few very specific keywords for your campaign, then the list might have been so small and so specific that no one was searching those keywords while you were running your campaign.

If you tried a few different types of sales copy plus a long list of keywords and still nothing, ask yourself: is my book relevant to the audience I'm trying to target? If your book is a romance but your keywords are targeting action adventure books, Amazon isn't going to feature your ad.

If You Broke Even

You're getting close! You have a list that's long enough and maybe some ad sales copy that makes someone want to click on it to learn more. So where's the problem? There could be a few things going wrong, but odds are you need to refine your keyword list and make adjustments to your bid amount.

Adjusting Bids Based on Placement

If you visit the "Placements" tab of your campaign you'll be able to see where your ad is showing up. Your ad can be placed in any of the three spots:

- Top of search—The first page of search results
- Product pages—Another book's sales page
- Rest of search—A search result page that isn't the first page

You'll be able to see the number of impressions for each spot and if you notice you aren't getting as many impressions in one of the spots, you have the ability to adjust your bid amount for that placement. For example, I noticed one of my ads wasn't getting placement on the first page of search results so I increased the bid by 2%. Just small changes like this can make a big difference.

Adjusting Bids Based on Keywords

If you need to change keywords, you can do that under the "Targeting" tab. This will tell you what keywords were the ones that caused you to get clicks. You'll also have the option to edit individual bids here. When I look at my individual keywords, I like to sort them by the number of clicks so the keywords with the most clicks will be displayed at the top. See what the ACOS (advertising costs of sales) is for each keyword. If the percentage is higher than 25% I'd suggest lowering your bid amount.

If you find that one keyword is getting good clicks and sales, try to add similar keywords. For example, if the keyword that is performing well is a book, find other comp titles to that book and add it to your list of keywords.

On the other hand, if you find a lot of people are clicking on a keyword but not buying, consider deleting that keyword because the audience for that keyword may not be a good fit for your book.

Optimizing Lock Screen Ads

So far we've really only talked about optimizing Sponsored Product Ads, but let's not forget how to optimize the Lock Screen ads. The process for optimizing lock screen ads is simpler because while most of what I've already said will apply to lock screen ads, such as knowing when to change your bid amount, you don't have a lot of keywords to sift through and compare. In the above scenarios, instead of changing or adjusting your keywords, you'll only need to adjust your genre.

One Last Trick To Give Your Ad a Boost

Like I've said, Amazon loves ads that get good engagement and are a perfect fit for customers.

Besides targeting your ad correctly, there is another way you can have Amazon promote your ad without having to increase your bid, and that's by optimizing your book's sales page. Whatever keywords you use to target your ad should also show up on your book's page in these areas:

- **The book's description**— The last paragraph of the book description could be something along the lines of, "A young adult contemporary about…"
- **The book's title or subtitle**—This is why you'll sometimes see even fiction with a title, followed by a subtitle like, "A Young Adult Contemporary."

- **Inside the book**—Amazon can see inside your book if you publish through KDP, which means they can use that information to analyze your book as well. If your book is fiction, an easy way to sneak in keywords is by putting a very short description in the copyright page of your book.

If you write non-fiction, odds are your keywords will show up seamlessly throughout the book, as well as the book's title and description, but it's still something you can keep in mind if you feel like your book is lacking keywords.

Adding New Keywords

Popularity of books change on a regular basis. When we created our keyword list, we added books that were ranking in the top 20 spots for their genre, but this list of books is constantly changing. If you feel like your list of keywords needs new life added to them, re-visit the genres of your book and add in any additional books in the top rankings.

BETHANY'S TIPS:

I know I said this in the previous chapter, but it bears repeating: learning how to do ads well takes time!

Successful paid marketing can be summed up like this:

1. Knowing your ideal reader like you know yourself

2. Setting the book itself up for success with a good cover, title, blurb, etc., and...

3. Not being afraid to try and fail

Obviously, this is very simplistic, and actually completing each of these steps is hard. Not to mention, emotional. Failing isn't easy. But remember, successful people fail more than anybody else. The difference is, they don't let those failures stop them.

Like C.S. Lewis says, "You can let failure stop you, or you can fail forward toward success." Take these strategies one at a time—remember the advice from book one about choosing your top three focuses—and then dive in. You've got this!

CHAPTER 11:
CELEBRATE YOURSELF

"You can't let perfection get in the way of

getting things done."

– Gini Dietrich

ADS DON'T HAVE to be hard and they don't have to cost a lot of money. Authors produce phenomenal stories, but they're afraid to invest in them.

Bethany and I want to remind you that you published a book, you've gotten this far, so take that extra step and promote your book. Tell the world why they need to read your story.

Why do traditionally published books sell better than self-published books? There are a handful of reasons, but one huge reason is because many traditional publishers have a whole team to promote a book. You're just one person already doing so much, so it can feel daunting to try to learn something else like book marketing, but your time and effort will be worth it. As a self-published author, you have the power to sell your books just as well as big-name publishing companies. Will it take more work? Yes. Will it take you longer to get there? Probably. The road to success is yours, and when you get there nothing will feel better than being able to say that *you* did it. Nothing is stopping your book from becoming a best-seller. Have faith in yourself and try new things.

You have control to make this book and every book you write a success.

This book has given you the knowledge and the tools to lead new readers to your book, so go find them.

In the end, it all comes down to marketing your book to your ideal reader. If you market your book to the masses you waste time, energy and money. Find the perfect reader for your book and think of them each time you market your book.

THANKS FOR READING!

Please leave a short review on Amazon to let us know what you thought!

RESOURCES:

Here are some links from each of the chapters that we think you might find valuable!

Bethany's "Book Marketing for Authors" YouTube Playlist:

http://bit.ly/bookmarketingforauthors

Mandi's "Marketing for Authors" YouTube Playlist: http://bit.ly/MandisNews

Chapter 1 (Your Ideal Reader)

- Ideal Reader Profile Printable:

  http://bit.ly/MandisNews

Chapter 2 (Creating Graphics & Sales Copy)

- Adobe's Color Tool

  https://color.adobe.com/create
- Book Brush

  https://bookbrush.com/
- Book Brush Facebook Group

  https://www.facebook.com/groups/BookBrush/
- Create 3D rendering of your book

  www.diybookcovers.com/3Dmockups/

Chapter 3 (Newsletter Swaps & Features)

- 20Booksto50K Facebook Group

  https://www.facebook.com/groups/20Booksto50k/
- Author Newsletter Share and Swap

  https://www.facebook.com/groups/authornewsletterswap/

- Romance Authors Newsletter Swap

    https://www.facebook.com/groups/RomanceAuthorsNewsletterSwapandCrossPromo/
- Author Newsletter Swap and Cross Promo

    https://www.facebook.com/groups/802170179946656/
- StoryOrigin

    https://storyoriginapp.com/
- BookBoast

    https://www.bookboast.com/
- AXP Newsletter Swap Club

    https://authorsxp.com/swap
- Bit.ly for link tracking

    https://app.bitly.com/

Chapter 4 (eBook Promotion Sites)

- BookBub

    https://www.bookbub.com/
- BookBub Pricing and Sales Estimate

    https://www.bookbub.com/partners/pricing-

Websites Similar to BookBub:

- Awesomegang

    https://awesomegang.com/
- Book Cave

    https://mybookcave.com/
- BookSends

    https://booksends.com/
- Book Sliced

    https://booksliced.com/
- Bookperk

    http://www.bookperk.com/
- Books Butterfly

    https://www.booksbutterfly.com/
- eBook Soda

    http://www.ebooksoda.com/
- eReader News Today

    https://ereadernewstoday.com/
- FreeBooksy

    https://www.freebooksy.com/
- Kindle Nation Daily

    https://kindlenationdaily.com/

- Genre Pulse

    https://www.genrepulse.com/
- GoodKindles

    https://www.goodkindles.net/
- Reading Deals

    https://readingdeals.com/
- Robin Reads

    https://robinreads.com/
- The Fussy Librarian

    https://www.thefussylibrarian.com/

Free Book Feature Websites:

- Author Marketing Club

    https://authormarketingclub.com/
- Babs Book Bistro

    https://babsbookbistro.net/
- Bargin Booksy

    https://www.bargainbooksy.com/
- BookCircleOnline

    https://www.bookcircleonline.com/
- Book Raid

https://bookraid.com/
- E Reader Girl

    https://ereadergirl.com/
- Daily Bookworm

    http://thedailybookworm.com/
- Digital Book Today

    https://digitalbooktoday.com/
- Indie Author News

    https://www.indieauthornews.com/
- Inkitt

    https://www.inkitt.com/
- Pretty Hot Books

    https://pretty-hot.com/

Chapter 8 (Collecting Data For Amazon Ads)

- Publisher Rocket

    https://publisherrocket.com/
- Stone Ridge Books, Book Cover Design

    https://stoneridgebooks.com/book-cover-design/

ABOUT THE AUTHORS

ABOUT: MANDI

Mandi Lynn published her first novel when she was seventeen. The author of *Essence*, *I am Mercy* and *She's Not Here*, Mandi spends her days continuing to write and creating YouTube videos to help other writers achieve their dreams of seeing their books published. Mandi is the owner of Stone Ridge Books, a company that works to help authors bring their books to life through cover design and digital book marketing. She is also the creator of AuthorTube Academy, a course that teaches authors how to grow their presence on YouTube and find loyal readers. When she's not creating, you can find Mandi exploring her backyard or getting lost in the woods.

BOOKS BY MANDI:

CONNECT WITH MANDI ON:

Website: https://mandilynn.com

Instagram: @mandilynnwrites

Facebook: @mandilynnwrites

Twitter: @mandilynnwrites

YouTube: www.youtube.com/mandilynnVLOGS

Goodreads: Mandi Lynn

AuthorTube Academy: bit.ly/AuthorTube

AuthorTube Academy Facebook Group: http://bit.ly/2JhamHY

Mandi's Patreon: http://bit.ly/2NnhXa6

ABOUT: BETHANY

Bethany Atazadeh is a Minnesota-based author of YA novels, children's books, and non-fiction. She graduated from Northwestern College in 2008 with a Bachelor of Arts degree in English with a writing emphasis. After graduation, she pursued songwriting, recording, and performing with her band, and writing was no longer a priority. But in 2016, she was inspired by the

NaNoWriMo challenge to write a novel in 30 days, and since then she hasn't stopped. With her degree, she coaches other writers on both YouTube and Patreon, helping them write and publish their books. She is obsessed with stories, chocolate, and her corgi puppy, Penny.

BOOKS BY BETHANY

CONNECT WITH BETHANY ON:

Website: www.bethanyatazadeh.com

Instagram: @authorbethanyatazadeh

Facebook: @authorbethanyatazadeh

Twitter: @bethanyatazadeh

YouTube: www.youtube.com/bethanyatazadeh

Goodreads: Bethany Atazadeh

Patreon: www.patreon.com/bethanyatazadeh

Printed in Great Britain
by Amazon